The Great Py...

How it was ... than 7 ...

MindStrength International

www.MindStrength.info

Authors

Leon Tunney-Ware & Mervyn L. Johnson

About the Authors

Leon Tunney-Ware:
Has worked in the field of Personal Development for the past 20 years and is a quailified Hypnotist as well as a writer.

Leon studied under Ormond McGill who wrote 'The New Encyclopedia of Stage Hypnotism Hypnotism' and is recognised as 'The Dean of American Hypnotists' a world leader in his his field. Leon has been involved in writng for the past 20 years on various topics mainly on problem solving.

He also has various outside business interests. Married with 10 children and lives on his country estate on the west coast of southern Ireland.

Mervyn L. Johnson:
Works alongside Leon in the field of Personal Development and was trained by Leon in the same field. Mervyn and Leon came together in the early 90's to write their first book and to form their company MindStrength Int.
He moved to Cambridge from London in 1995 where he continues to reside.

Mervyn also has other outside business interests, And has 2 daughters and 3 grandchildren.

Dedications

Our thanks go to Ros, Bonny and our families for all their support, patience and understanding.

Also our thanks go to Bill, Mandy, & Denise

Simple Solutions to a 4,500 Year Mystery

By Leon Tunney-Ware & Mervyn L. Johnson

Table of Contents

About the Authors 5
Dedications 7
Introduction 12
The Mystique Surrounding the Pyramids 13
There are many Theories 14
A Higher Power 16
Were the Ancient Egyptians more Advanced? .. 17
The Logistics of a 20 Year Timeframe 32
Clear Line of Thought 36
Irrational Logic 39
Logistics of the Build 40
A Transparent Perspective 41
Facts 42
Other Factors 46
How is this Possible? 48
Harnessing the Force of Gravity 53
Built in less than 7 years 54
Preparing the Foundation 55
Excavation of the Foundations 58
Levelling the Foundation 62
Our Solution to Levelling the Base 64
Outer Perimeter is Squared and Marked 67
The Datum Wall 68
Transportation of the Stone Blocks 70
How the Embankment Ramps were Utilised 71
The Datum Wall is then Erected 73
Datum Rulers 75
How the 52 Degree Angle was Maintained 76

How were the Blocks Levelled? 78
How the Blocks were Laid 80
The Technique used to Place the Blocks...........83
The Mechanics.. 88
Structure Takes Shape.....................................89
Giant Obstacle 91
The Queens Chamber 93
The Kings Chamber 94
Grand Gallery 96
90% Completed within 29 Months....................98
Previous Theories Prove Impractical 103
Our solution.. 105
Summary 108
MindStrength.info... 110

INTRODUCTION

We believe that our book offers an insight into the reality of how the Great Pyramid of Giza was actually constructed. By using simple, yet logical and time saving methods the ancient Egyptians actually completed this imposing monument in less than 7 years.

The Khufu Pyramid has been a source of mystery for 4,500 years. An enigma seated on the Giza plateau retaining a host of untold secrets of its true origin and construction. Over time numerous varied theories have been documented in the hope of unravelling the mystique surrounding the pyramids.

When you consider the ancient Egyptians, their lifestyle, culture, religious beliefs and the mortality rate, it leaves very little manoeuvrability within the notion that it took 20 years to construct. Time was of the essence.

The Khufu Pyramid's construction methods are open to question as there are no records or plans available to give an exact blueprint of the build and the procedures used.

We can only apply common sense and best judgement to date to qualify its existence.

The Mystique Surrounding the Pyramids

There are a variety of theories on how the pyramids were built. But do they categorically give the solution whereby, it's possible to replicate their magnificent accomplishment in today's digital age? Even in the 21st century mind it's believed their task to be so incomprehensible with the tools they used that some people in our society are convinced that the pyramids were actually built by aliens!

This may seem extreme when you cast your mind back to those ancient times as they didn't possess any so-called modern machinery. Yet these majestic structures the Egyptians built were so massively impressive and remained the tallest man-made structures until the early nineteen hundreds. So what was so awe inspiring about their feats?

Why is it perceived such a baffling problem to build the pyramids? Was it their overall height, the angles? If the structures had been 50ft. high with a base of 50 ft. square would it have been so wondrous? Would we continue to marvel at their achievements? Possibly not so much. The Great Pyramid of Giza is the largest of all the pyramids and is considered to be one of the 7 wonders of the world.

There are many Theories

The structure dictates and supports many of to-day's theories. All we can really do with hindsight is logically examine the apparent facts to the best of our ability to unravel this giant puzzle.

By analysing a combination of some of the best ideas surrounding the pyramid to date combined with a clear perspective.

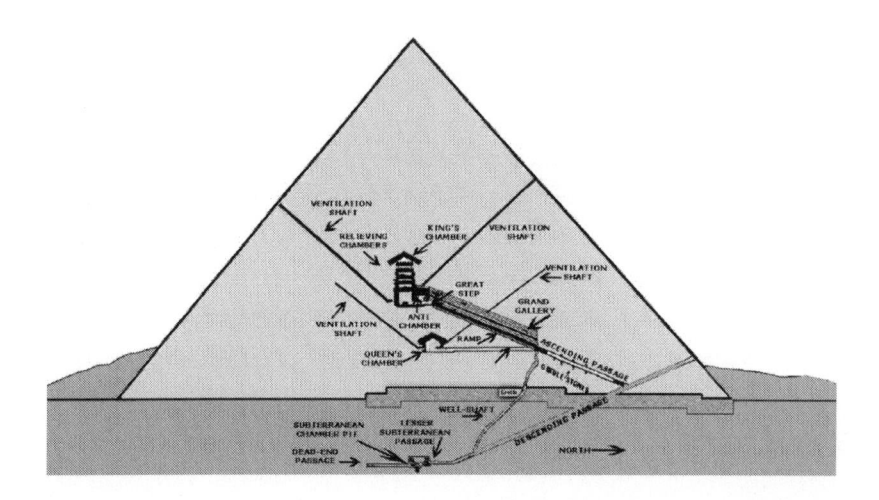

A logical solution to a cryptic problem can be found to reveal a blueprint to describe the existence of these grand monuments. There are numerous ideas to filter through we won't bore you with the mechanics within the analysis.

Included in some of the theories it is indicated that up the outer sides (faces) of the pyramid a type of track and pulley system was used to transport the heavy blocks and materials to the required level.

The track and pulley system was extended as each level was laid. Then there is the notion that a ramp was fashioned in a spiral around the pyramid enabling them to move these huge blocks to their destination.

Another theory suggested that the pyramid was built from the inside out with an internal ramp leaving out the corners of each side to enable transportation of materials and the open corners were completed later.

And then there is the long ramp theory whereby, a ramp was erected approx. a mile long to reach the top of the pyramid and some believe it would have taken longer to construct the ramp than the pyramid.

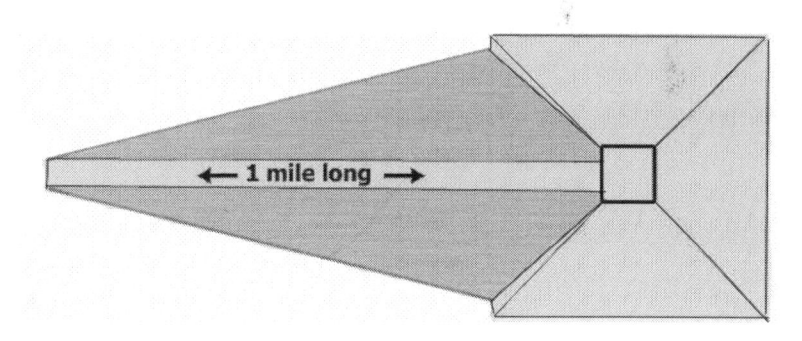

And then we have what some would call the extreme that an alien race built these impressive structures.

A Higher Power

The value of information falls into distinct realms: God, Aliens, Mythical creatures or Humans, the significance of which is, if you believe it to be impossible for a human then what options are available?
How you evaluate the existence of the pyramids is determined by which realm you fall into.

If you believe in God, and all things are possible, then after all other avenues are exhausted you can justify that God manifested the pyramids. This would be a simple task considering that God made the universe in 7 days. Or in fact all Pharaohs were Gods and *they* manifested the pyramids.

However, if you have a vague or no belief in God, your options are that of giants or mythical creatures or simply the Egyptians were a highly developed civilisation.
Now we are not trying to discredit any existing theories or beliefs all we're aiming to do is to simplify the mystique and bring it into the human realm.

Were the Ancient Egyptians more Advanced?

Is it truly a fact that the ancient Egyptians were more advanced than today's modern age? If so is it because of their race, their culture? Has that continued throughout time? Is their way of thinking on a higher level today? I.e. technically more advanced, plainly not.

On average we are all very similar as a human race in today's standing, so did the ancient Egyptians lose something along the timeline 'till the present day?
Based on the modern consensus you would have to surmise this is the status quo. Yet as a modernistic society we are still in awe of their achievements, so we are back to the question how were the pyramids built 4,500 years ago?

To have clarity of judgement you must first remove all data that is inferior or misleading and recognise any variables that could misguide you. With this done the obvious can be recognised, the obvious being the truth.

Not the truth as we know it because our individual truth is unique to ourselves to a point we believe at times we are so correct yet the complete opposite could be true. The framework of our intelligence is based upon the information we

give value to and the consistencies within our information that creates our individual truth.

So what is it, in the 21st century that creates, we
believe, this enigmatic perception about constructing the pyramids? Whereby it appears so
impossible to build that after 45 centuries there
is still no simple solution or clear blueprint as to
how these monuments were actually constructed.

To the extreme that some in our society surmise
that aliens created them or that the ancient Egyptians were more advanced 4,500 years ago than
we are today.
Were the Ancient Egyptians truly more intelli-
gent, more progressive? As mentioned the
consensus within society seems to be so, only because in today's age we believe we could not
replicate those magnificent structures with the
tools of their time.

So logical reasoning would indicate that they
were technically more advanced than us.
But is this truly the case?

You must remember your perception of reality is
your reality your perceptions of the facts are your
facts. Whatever you believe to be true automatically creates a pattern of thought that restricts
and governs your thinking to the extent that anything above, below or parallel is also true.

To put this into context, if you know that the maximum weight you can lift is 20 kg then this sets a benchmark because automatically now you are aware that you cannot lift anything heavier.

However, the benchmark also reflects that anything lighter than 20 kg is possible for you to lift. For further clarity, the current world record for running the men's 1500m is 3.26 minutes which is just less than a mile.

If this is the best that's believed can be achieved then logically speaking the average man is unable to run the same distance in the same time. Automatically creating beliefs that are parallel to this fact the only variable in this example is, could the average man run a quarter of this distance (375m) in less than a quarter of the time 51.50 seconds?

You would surmise it's possible because clearly a runner tires over longer distances. To highlight the point the men's hundred metre world record stands at 9.58 sec, if we multiply this time by 15 it would equate to a time of 2minutes 23seconds a quarter of this time equates to 36.92seconds.

This proves that it is possible to run a quarter of 1500m in less than a quarter of the time. We can't accurately predict the time it would take the average man to run 375m but we can predict that

it's possible to run it faster than a minute. In essence the same runner who ran 1500mts in 3.26 minutes could not run 3000 mts. in 6.52 minutes.
All the above times and distances are for a male runner as we said previously for one thing to be true anything above below or parallel is also true.

To help the penny drop further could a woman equal or better the above examples. The consistencies within society's beliefs suggest not. We are not implying this is the case we are only stating the average beliefs within society. It is believed the male is stronger and faster than the female automatically creating parallel thoughts.

The consistencies within these thoughts manifest the facts creating societies perception that it's illogical to accept that a woman can run quicker than a man.

That's the problem with the mind it's very linear in how it constructs our beliefs. It doesn't matter whether we as individuals disagree with our own internal thinking or the consistencies of the thinking within society it would appear that once your mind is made-up, it's made-up. And our thoughts are set in stone.
There are those within society that occasionally set the trend and our thinking, in a way, upgrades however following the norm.

Each belief is very similar to the structure of the pyramid. The top stone of the pyramid representing the hierarchy belief-fact and the subsequent levels and the blocks they contain are our supporting beliefs-facts that are in line and parallel with each other. Not necessarily consistent with each other because the variable is value.

For the mind to be able to comprehend, articulate, evaluate, judge and determine right from wrong, fact from fiction it has to have a consistent base line of value that is calibrated based on its own unique personal perception of the world.

As a society our uniqueness is compounded by the consistencies of other people's beliefs creating a universal calibrated baseline that we and others within our society interpret as the world we live in.
To clarify we'll use history as an example: the consistent facts are that any quantum leap our civilisation has taken, in many cases, has been as a consequence of the unique beliefs of particular individuals in time gone by and their ability to communicate their convictions.

For example: if you were to exclude 16 highly influential historical figures from history i.e.: the Wright brothers, Edison, Alexander Graham Bell, Isaac Newton, Einstein, Darwin, Freud, Benjamin Franklin, Abraham Lincoln, Churchill,

Hitler, Gandhi, Jesus, Buddha, Allah or even Henry VIII our world would be totally different. Very long winded we know but necessary.

How we think and perceive the world in our modern era is a consequence of the thinking of the above individuals and others of similar ilk.
The essential point is when you exclude these people from history todays' society would be totally different, along with our personal thinking and our perception of the world.

Some of you reading this book possibly know very little about the pyramids and are just reading out of interest and your mind won't be caught up with the conjecture surrounding this topic.
However, there are those reading this book that have all the facts and theories within their mindset.
The book we are writing is not to debate the mindset surrounding the construction or the existence of the pyramids it is only to give a clear perspective.

You might think the above is not congruent with the subject to hand but let's put it another way take the pharaohs beliefs out of the equation and would the pyramids exist? They simply wouldn't.
If the ancient Egyptians were actually an advanced civilisation what that equates to is, they thought differently than us. They had different beliefs and priorities.

In our opinion to fully understand how the pyramids were built you have to take a different perspective than the norm. And step back from the aura that these tombs have created throughout history and allow your mind to default back to its infancy where it had no facts just curiosity and it judged everything on its own merit and made up its own mind.

Automatically removing conjecture and believed facts and take the structure of the pyramid down to its simplest form where it's literally one block on top of another. And recognising that the only natural force in our universe to date that creates the mystique surrounding these monuments is gravity.

It's not the height of the structure it's not the angles in the structure it's the imposing universal force of gravity. Ask the wrong question i.e. "how do you get the top block to the top of the pyramid" and your mind will create the solution to the best of its ability.

Ask the question "what stops the top block from being laid at the height of 481ft?" your mind does the same thing it goes to work to find a solution.

The questions you debate in your mind create a structure of thoughts/beliefs/facts that are consistent with each other and are opposite to each other.

The mind has what it believes to be possible and to be impossible, what is fact, what is fiction etc. The problem with how the mind evaluates, analyses and values the information can sometimes systematically create false perceptions of reality.

The mind cannot analyse or perceive anything beyond what it believes to be true. What the mind believes to be possible, automatically creating what it perceives to be impossible:
'As man thinketh so shall he be' or another way 'according to your beliefs let it be done unto you'.

The sting in the tail, for want of a better word, is that many of us subscribe to the exact same beliefs automatically creating what we perceive to be reality 'the world we live in' when in fact the opposite could be the absolute truth.

Based on our understanding of the world and to what level we are educated and our self-value and where we fit into society's structures, our own mind learns not to think, not to question, because we believe others to be more capable. So how does this relate to the building of the pyramids?

The significance is to outline how the human race processes and evaluates information. Of course no two individuals think identically however, there are core elements that make us somewhat a clone of each other whereby even though we are a race of many cultures our thinking is similar, regardless of race, language or sex.

For centuries even the best scholars throughout history have marvelled at how these structures were built yet you would think after 4,500 years a simple straightforward explanation would be documented.

However, the consensus is the ancient Egyptians were a more advanced civilization.
But if we comprehend that to be true then automatically a process of reasoning follows suit and compounds our assessment of our perceived facts and we blinker ourselves from a simple, sound explanation.

As we said previously for one thing to be true then anything above, below or parallel is also true. By perceiving the Egyptians were of a more advanced culture or that an alien species built the pyramids the parameters of the problem are automatically set.

Our beliefs systematically create a solution to how these structures were erected. The answer, in essence is *they were* more advanced, indicating we are inferior and incapable of solving the problem. So all we can do is wonder and theorise.

A Neutral Perspective

For us to transparently assess these structures we must default to a neutral playing field of bare logic and only assess the facts with personalities and egos' aside looking at the bare-bones of the problem.

It is believed the Great Pyramid of Giza was built in the fourth dynasty for the Pharaoh Khufu, or his Hellenized name Cheops.

It is documented that he reigned for approx. 23 years around the year 2580BC. However, there is supposition about the length of his reign.

The original size of this 7th wonder is thought to be 481ft but today it stands at 455.4ft. It remained the tallest man-made construction until the completion of the Eiffel tower which stands 1,050 ft. The total mass of the Khufu Pyramid is estimated to be 5.8 million tonnes. It's widely theorised that the construction took around 20 years.

So if it took 20 years to complete and the mass weight is 5.8m tonnes then to enable them to finish within this time-frame they would have to install 795 tons of stone per 12 hour day. This equates to laying approx. 66.20 tons per hour which denotes they had to lay approx. 1.10 tons per minute. The average weight of each block was 2.5 tons the average size of each block is 5x8x12ft.

So at this rate they quarried, hauled, delivered and placed each block in an average timeframe of 2 minutes and 16 seconds.

An amazing achievement even by modern day standards when you consider a good brick-layer can lay on average 1.5 bricks per minute, 90 bricks per hour 720 per 8 hour day when he has everything to hand.

Keep in mind that the modern day brick-layer is only laying each brick and would not be expected to make, transport, and deliver as well as lay each brick.

You could argue with sound judgement that it was possible to lay each 2.5 ton block in an average time frame of 2 minutes and 16 seconds because it is understood that the Egyptians had thousands of people working on the site at any given time.

Bear in mind there are no hard facts to support that the Khufu Pyramid was completed within 20 years, only theories. Others are of the opinion it was completed within a shorter timetable of 14 years which is even more extraordinary.

And this is without taking into account any ground-works i.e. levelling the foundation, excavating down to the subterranean levels and quarrying materials.

Metals for any tools had to be sourced and forged, timber had to be harvested for use as rollers, sledges and wedges etc. materials for ropes had to be sourced and worked, and the list is endless.

And we haven't even touched on the human element, the workforce... Try and imagine the number of people that would have been required to achieve such an outstanding accomplishment. The skills necessary along with tradesmen, labourers, and in addition we have to take into account their basic needs: food, water, shelter, latrines etc. Never mind the complications involved in the routine running of such a grandiose project.

Then you have the consequences on the health of the workforce due to the build with the effects of the dust, debris, and the blazing heat, along with the number of injuries and deaths that must have occurred. And we cannot disregard the everyday general health factors, such as disease, sickness, diarrhoea etc.

Days lost due to sickness would have taken its toll. We estimate that approx. 10% of the workforce could have been out of action due to sickness throughout each year. That's 100 people in every 1000.

This figure may seem exaggerated but when you view a modern day equivalent it seems very conservative.

The statistics in 2011, of the average working person in the UK working in modern day conditions took approx. 5.2 days off sick. That's 5200 workdays lost per 1000 people each year due to sickness. You would envisage that in the 4th Dynasty, or thereabouts, the average would be higher.

All the above components are relative throughout a 20 year timetable. These are factors they would have considered at the planning stage and continued to be priorities throughout the timeline of the build.

Without taking into account all these components it would be impossible to construct the pyramid period, even if the timeline had been 40 years.

The biggest impact on the construction of the pyramid was the average life expectancy of the ancient Egyptian. This is estimated to be about 35 years. Yet considering their working environment you would deem their life expectancy to be shorter.

Why is this important? Age, fitness, experience are significant variables and would have had a dramatic impact on the construction if they were working with a 20 year timetable.

It's hard to imagine a 15 year old starting as a labourer because of the physical strength required. We think it more plausible to gauge the starting age of a labourer would be nearer to 20. As for the skilled worker stone masons etc. logically they would need to be older to have acquired the necessary essentials crafts.

And considering their working environment and health hazards it's reasonable to project the average life expectancy would be shorter than 35 years. Realistically indicating that the labourer had at best 15 working years ahead of him and a skilled worker 10.

The dilemma would be a diminishing workforce impacting on the overall productivity. With a working time frame of 20 years visibly these factors would have been calculated at the outset and contingencies would have been put in place.
With an on-going recruitment process across the lands of Egypt, training for the necessary skills and a form of health care etc.

Slaves v Workers

At this point we're sure you'd agree an extremely large workforce would be needed. It's thought that a large number of the workers were slaves, this is entirely possible.

However, slave-labour would be too inconsistent for the task in hand. Productivity would be affected because of low morale, and pride in their work would be non-existent. Therefore the use of slave labour would be too unpredictable for a 20 year timetable.

We're not implying that slave labour wasn't used however, if it was part of the workforce then logically you would surmise it would have been on a smaller scale. Because this class of labour would require overseers and slave masters applying sheer brute force, dominant control coupled with psychological authority to increase productivity and quality of work.

This may be effective for short periods of time, but for 20 years? Not unless they were treated as mere animals and they served their purpose until such time their purpose was served.

The hypothesis is that the life expectancy of a slave worker to be shorter than that of the average. The overall confidence for including this grade of workforce at the planning stage would conceivably be low and the target for completion in 20 years could be compromised.

The Logistics of a 20 Year Timeframe

You would expect specific instructions were conveyed to the architect partnered with a timeframe for completion.

Considering that the average life expectancy was more or less 35 years the construction would have to be completed before the death of the Pharaoh.

There are no actual records to confirm the pharaoh's age but it has been documented he reigned for about 23 years, besides which there are no accurate records when construction commenced.

Throughout the whole planning process the architect and his team had to consider every minute detail. They firmly recognised the time constraints against them in building this vast monument.

They could not allow everyday circumstances to impose on the productivity nothing, could be left to chance.

Now remember the previous calculation of 2.5 tons installed every 136 seconds is the consistent average over a 20 year time frame.

That equates to every worker working non-stop for 12 hours a day 7 days a week, 52 weeks of the year for a total of 20 years.

Regardless of the number of people working on the project there is still a stage where the possible becomes the impossible. Now consider the average person walks 1 mile (5280ft) in approx. 15 minutes and the base of the pyramid is 755ft in length (divide 5280ft by 755ft = 7 times approx.).

For the average person to walk this distance on ground level with a clear path and not carrying or pulling anything would take them approximately 2 minutes 8.5 seconds.

You also need to keep in mind that's just the length of the pyramid, as each level rises the distance becomes longer and the task becomes harder as they have to manoeuvre the blocks *uphill*.

So the more you contemplate the 20 year time frame with a block being installed every 2m 16s the more ludicrous it becomes.

To be reasonable and realistic we'll give you a modern day example: A delivery truck arrives loaded with 10 blocks of stone with a combined weight of 25 tons approx. size of each stone is 5x8ft.x12ft. He has a machine to unload the lorry and transport the stone on a level surface 755ft to its destination, the machine driver positions the block into place then returns to the lorry. This process continues until all 10 blocks are in place and the exercise is completed in 22 minutes and 40 seconds (2m 16s per block)

The same timeframe the Egyptians had to quarry, transport and place 10 blocks, with a combined weight of 25 tons, average size of each stone 5x8x12ft working a 12 hour shift.
Now remember in our above example we haven't quarried or delivered the stone, sourced any tools, or worked in dusty conditions under the hot, baking sun.

We've just used a modern day scenario to rein-force how impossible it appears to achieve its past equivalent without machinery. So let's say they worked a full 24 hour day. The first shift worked 12 hours followed by the second working the nightshift which would require double the workforce, best they could achieve on average would be 4 minutes 32 seconds per 2.5 ton block.

You would suspect the second shift to work slow-er as their visibility would be restricted. The task is still not palatable. It's still in the realms of im-possibility and the more you deliberate the greater the time expectancy of 20 years defies logic.

This is without taking into account Mother Na-ture imposing her wrath with sand-storms, flooding, drought and famine etc. all taking their toll over the 20 year timeframe.
To overcome the problem we could just simply extend the timeframe.

Let's double it or better still triple it. Now we have 60 years to complete the task which equates to 6 minutes and 48 seconds per block working a 12 hour day.
Or working a 24 hour shift we have 13 min and 36 sec to quarry, transport and lay each stone. It's just not quite digestible yet.

At this point we can understand why some people theorise that the pyramids were the mark of an alien species. Dependant on your viewpoint one could rationalise that the more humanly impossible the task appears, the more we have to look to a higher power.

Clear Line of Thought

To find a solution to any problem you must first have a clear line of thought. Bear in mind the problem we are looking to solve is 4,500 years old. That in itself is probably the biggest problem of all, *why?*
45 centuries is an extremely long period. Imagine the billions of people that have walked the earth throughout that time-frame and the many that have contemplated these magnificent structures. *And there is still no conclusive blueprint?* Astounding really.

An ancient Rubik's Cube, a towering enigma, which has stood the test of time. You need to re-alise the Egyptians wouldn't have built the pyramids if they didn't know how. The problem is not how they were built but rather how to de-cipher what *they* knew. That is why a clear line of thought is necessary.

So we need to establish a baseline of fact, to transparently view the obstacles the Egyptians had to overcome. To do this we must first verify where the challenges lie.
We can obviously assume that the size and height of the structure had been pre-determined during the planning stage. Based on the pyramid's sym-metrical features a suitable site location was

chosen, close to the source of stone and materials which would facilitate the build.

When the symmetry of the structure was established it clearly indicated the potential difficulties that lay ahead. Undoubtedly the terrain was surveyed to ensure a solid foundation that could support such an edifice.
A system of excavation would be involved in choosing the location i.e. trial holes to determine the suitability of the site. Their first obstacle to overcome would be excavating the site by removing any rocks, blocks, sand and debris.

It has been documented that the site of the Great Pyramid of Giza was built on a granite base which would have required levelling. Irrefutably an extremely difficult task at that time with the tools they had to hand, but not impossible.
The two main obstacles at the foundation level, one would have been working the granite to form a level base.

The second to surmount was, resolving the base level over such a vast area, realising the base of the Khufu Pyramid covers 13 acres, 570025sq ft. approx. the area of 8 football pitches.

It's been documented that an outer wall was erected surrounding the perimeter base of the pyramid to help overcome the challenge of levelling this vast area.

It is believed the perimeter wall was built so they could flood the entire base of the pyramid to determine the level of the foundation.

We presume this theory is better than aliens building the pyramid but it's just one of those ideas that just does not concur with the time constraints. Without arguing the point we must remember they supposedly had 20 years from start to finish.

The problem with logic is you can sometimes paint yourself into a corner with an idea and allow the idea to dictate and initiate a conception of thought that's perceived logical but is in fact irrational.

Some of the theories to date are very well thought through and have substance.

However, there are theories that portray substance but in fact when analysed they are just stepping blocks of information that have been conjured up to be perceived fact.

Irrational Logic

By using the example of the perimeter wall, which was erected so they could flood the area to enable them to level the base. It can be seen as a logical solution to a difficult problem, however, the substance within this form of logic is irrational and we'll explain why....

The problem is dictating its own solution because of one fact. It's been documented that the first accurate levelling device was invented long after the pyramids were built.

With this information thinking becomes blinkered. At the same time you have the obvious fact that the structure exists and its foundation was obviously levelled in one way or another, these two facts are not congruent with each other and become stepping stones within the thought process hindering a simple solution.
Rather than seeking a simpler solution a more complex idea-theory has to evolve.

Never mind the complexities of the task or the time constraints involved, we'll push that to the side. Let's not get caught up with conjecture, let's move on.

Logistics of the Build

We are certain you'll agree that an immense amount of fore-thought would have gone into a project of these proportions.
There are several avenues of thought we can use to decipher how the structure was built, each have their pros and cons. We can view it from a reverse engineering mind-set or from a pre-build mind-set.

If we observe it from a reverse engineer mind-set there are a lot of clues and facts that will aid our quest. Yet at the same time it's easy to get lost in the mystique surrounding the Khufu Pyramid.

If we look at it from a pre-build mind-set and place ourselves in the architect's shoes we can do our best to understand the many challenges and the logistics involved prior to the commencement of any work.

This process of thinking helps to better articulate the complexities of the problem. Nonetheless this line of deliberating will not give us the full facts.
It's all conjecture, we can only do our utmost accepting a hybrid combination of the two mind-sets is our best line of thought.

A Transparent Perspective

You would envisage at the design-planning stages all the components of the build were decided upon.

The design created the obstacles the architects, builders and engineers had to overcome. Bear in mind the Khufu Pyramid is of a similar design to other pyramids apart from the internal passage ways and chambers.
It is verified that it was common practise for Pharaohs to be entombed beneath their pyramid. However, the Khufu Pyramid was of a more complex design.
It houses the Kings Chamber, Queens's Chamber, the Grand Gallery plus passageways and four air-shafts. These create different challenges within the building structure.

To reverse engineer the complexity of the build we need to establish with certainty the facts we know to be true, and use these facts as the building blocks to establish the existence of the said structure.

Facts

The base area was approximately 13 acres, the length of each side was originally approximately 755ft. The original height was 481ft the tallest of all known pyramids, built on a consistent angle of 52 degrees with the entrance approximately 55ft from the base.

The number of blocks used has been calculated at 2,300,000 with an average weight of 2.5tons per block and the mass of the pyramid estimated to be around 5.8 million tons.

The blocks mainly consisted of granite and limestone. 1cubic metre is approx. 2.5tons. The average size of the blocks was 5x8x12ft. However the blocks varied in size.

The large granite blocks used in the Relieving Chambers above the Kings Chamber are believed to be in excess of 40-50 tons, possibly weighing as much as 80 tons.

The Kings Chamber is approximately 40 mts above base level. It is established there are 2 air shafts in the Kings Chamber which some refer to as spiritual openings.

Outside the Kings Chamber there is the Anti-Chamber which housed the portcullis blocks which were used to block the entrance to the King's Chamber. This leads onto the Grand Gallery which is 28ft in height by 153ft in length and is on a downward slope.

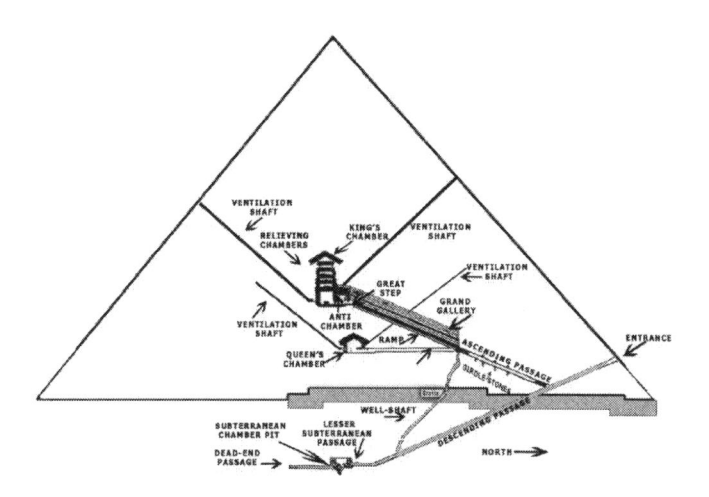

At the bottom of the Grand Gallery heading east is the horizontal Queens passage leading to the Queens Chamber which is exactly in the centre point between the north and south faces of the pyramid.

The Chamber measures approx. 18x17ft and houses an apex roof. In the north and south walls there are 2 air shafts which do not reach the outer side of the pyramid.

Now back at the bottom of the Grand Gallery heading north we have the Ascending passage. Also near the bottom of the Grand Gallery is the Well Shaft that leads down past the Grotto and continues into the subterranean levels which houses the subterranean Chamber.

Within this Chamber lays a pit approx. 60ft deep. Heading up from the subterranean levels north you have the descending passageway leading to the entrance.

43

In the early 19th century boat pits were discovered in the bedrock of the eastern and southern sides of the Khufu Pyramid. The 1224 pieces of one of the boats discovered on the southern side has been reassembled and now resides in the Khufu Boat Museum.

The Khufu ship is recognised as the oldest ship in history it measures 143 ft. long and 19.5ft wide and its craftsmanship is considered as a masterpiece of woodwork. It's understood to have been used by Pharaoh Khufu in his lifetime and later buried to act as a symbolic vessel in his after-life journey.

When you think of the timeline of 4,500bc your mind may envisage primitive people with primitive skills in bare feet and loincloths but as you can see from the image of the Khufu ship this couldn't be further from reality.

Other Factors

A factor to take into the equation is the life span of the main architect. Because of the consequences on the construction if he were to die before completion. Only an architect of status and experience would have been chosen for such an important project.

The obvious question would be "at what age would such an honour be bestowed upon him?" You wouldn't picture the architect to be in his early 'teens, so how is this relevant? With supposedly a 20 year time frame they would have to take into account the repercussions on the construction if the architect were to die before its completion.

One of the most important facts that hasn't been considered is the sole purpose of the pyramid, a tomb, in which to secure the Pharaohs body and facilitate his soul's journey into the afterlife. The Pharaohs' beliefs and religion were the hierarchy factors without which the pyramids would not exist today. Within their religious beliefs is the answer that compounds the overall problem.

You cannot imagine the consequences if they fail to complete the Pharaohs resting place before his death. So the urgency to finish the Pyramid was imperative based on the above facts, time is of the essence. So it's illogical to accept the luxury of a 20 year timeframe or longer.

Their religious beliefs were the governing factor that created the essence that dictated the driving force and the timeframe throughout the whole project from beginning to end.

Encompassing this factuality it's inconceivable to work with a 20 year timeframe so there had to be practical solutions that shrink this timetable dramatically.

What would've been a valid timeframe?

As we have ascertained, their governing factors were religion and life expectancy of the pharaoh, therefore realistically they would've worked with a far shorter timeframe.

Farcical it may seem, however, logically they had no choice other than to complete the tomb for their pharaoh as quickly as possible to ensure his final resting place.

Therefore with sound judgement we have concluded that the Great Pyramid of Giza would have to be completed within a timeframe of *less than 7 years*.

How is this Possible?

You would imagine we would have to work with a much longer timeframe. If you analyse the structure and, without taking into account its sole purpose and the average life expectancy of the ancient Egyptian, time is irrelevant, whether it takes 10, 50 or 100 years.

That's been the problem because all the theories to date have been viewed with a reverse engineering mind-set to solve one problem: how was the pyramid built?

A reverse engineering mindset can blinker, and the overall outcome is theories, that have evolved in time-lines written in stone to align with the theories. It's a bit like putting the cart before the horse.

With a pre-build mindset distinctly time would have been the governing factor. And the pressure the time-line created for the architect, engineers etc. would have created the priorities to find simple practical solutions.

If they were to use ramps: be it an external spiral ramp or an internal spiral ramp or even a long ramp combined with a configuration of primitive hoist-cranes or winch devices which logically the mind accepts as the possible solution.

But then your back to the problem dictating the solution. If time was *not* a factor, and they had all the time in the world, then all theories to date would stand on their own merit.

However, when time is the key component these theories merely hinder and bottleneck the whole construction process making it impossible to build in a practical timeframe.

The reason this is relevant? Because it's the ramp's width that regulates how many blocks can be moved up at any one time. If it's an internal spiral ramp the width would have to be approx. 6ft-10ft, remember the average weight of each stone is 2.5 tons the number of men required to move such a weight would be at least 50, that's the equivalent of 1cwt per man.

With 2 men abreast and a line of 25 men it would be necessary to have at least 120ft working space plus the average length of the stone, 12ft. Also if they had men pushing the blocks the maximum that could be used behind would be three.

49

So the absolute minimum length of working area needed would be 132ft per stone. Operating this method would result in blocks being hauled uphill in convoy style to make best use of the ramps. With materials being transported, in this fashion, up through or on the outside of the pyramid, it would be very slow and cumbersome.

Consider also, with an internal or external spiral ramp all the blocks would have to turn corners resulting in a very time restrictive practice.

Once the workforces arrived at their destination their return trip would have to be by ropes on the outer side of the pyramid.

They could not return the way they arrived as the width of the ramp only offers enough space to transport the blocks. The same restrictions apply to any external ramp.

The long ramp creates similar problems and any ancient lifting or winch devices believed used would undoubtedly slow down the whole process extending any timeframe.

However fast the blocks are delivered determines the rate at which the pyramid can be built.

So for the pyramid to be built in a timeframe to realise its purpose the materials would have to be delivered as fast as humanly possible.

Remember over a 20 year period each block has to be transported, hauled up the pyramid and laid within 2 minutes and 16 seconds.

Regardless of whichever (current) ramp theory employed, it's their overall width restrictions that would have slowed down the whole construction. Never mind the time lost in constructing such ramps besides which the necessary skills required to build them.

Without complicating the matter further or arguing the overall beliefs surrounding the subject we won't add into the equation oxen, ass or horses. It is possible that animals were used in the heavy transportation however this type of thinking is not congruent with the consensus.

If animals were used they would not be practical on the internal or external spiral ramps only on the long ramp theory.

However, the same restrictions apply whereby the width of the ramp dictates the overall amount of materials that can be transported at any one time.

All present methods on how the Khufu Pyramid was constructed consume time and restrict the construction process compounding the overall timeline.

All theories to date cannot support a timeline of 20 years or shorter. With everything we've laid out to this point it would seem impossible to reduce the time frame to less than 7 years. Yet a shorter timeframe dramatically reduces the pressure of the average life expectancy and many of the problems that would have arisen during the build over a 20 year plus span. By analysing the logistics we are in the realms of impossibility.

A problem is only a problem if you don't have a feasible solution. We are convinced we have a practical and logical answer that justifies how the Khufu Pyramid was actually built in less than 7 years to realise its true purpose.

Harnessing the Force of Gravity

So what was the unique major determining factor that's been disregarded for 4,500 years that made it possible for the ancient Egyptians to build and complete the pyramids in a practical timeframe? The most powerful natural force working against the construction of the pyramids was gravity.

All the mechanics of the theories to date are all designed within the mind-set whereby they work against gravity rather than utilising its full force to the best of their ability.
At the planning stage of the Khufu Pyramid the architects and engineers would try to overcome every problem before it became one.

Gravity being their known Achilles heel, they would have had a solution whereby they would utilise this natural force to their advantage.
Because when you boil the pyramid down to its nuts and bolts this is the only natural force that creates the perception that this ancient man made 7th wonder of the world was impossible to build without modern machinery.

In our modern age we have machinery that helps us defy the force of gravity and overcome many of the obstacles that the ancient Egyptians faced.

How the Great Pyramid of Giza was built in less than 7 years

Simple Solutions to a 4,500 Year Mystery

We will now explain how we believe the Great Pyramid of Giza (The Khufu Pyramid) was actually constructed and completed in less than 7 years.

Our methods demonstrate that along with our logical working techniques and our specifically designed tools it was more practical and straightforward than ever imagined for the ancient Egyptians to construct pyramids.

Preparing the Foundation

The foundations of the pyramid as with any building, modern or ancient, has to be built upon a solid base. With such a huge construction as the pyramid it would, without doubt, have to follow the same guidelines. So obviously it cannot be built on sand or debris.

Therefore the site of the pyramid foundations would need to be prepared by removing any sand, debris, and rocks etc. down to a solid base.

We estimate the depth they had to dig down to was at least 65ft. Why we surmise this depth is because there is a reference to the Sphinx being buried in sand. The body of the Sphinx is 200ft long and 65ft tall.

From this we can surmise that the Sphinx was buried approximately 55-65ft deep. determining that it would be reasonable to suggest at the time of preparing the foundations they had to dig down a minimum of 65ft. by removing any sand, debris, and rocks etc. down to a solid base. (bedrock)

The 18th Dynasty King Thutmose IV (1479 BC 1425 BC), installed a plaque between the Sphinx's front paws, describing how, when he was a young Prince, he had gone hunting and fell asleep in the shade of the Sphinx's head.
Thutmose had a dream where Ra Hor-Akhty the sun God, talking through the Sphinx, spoke to him, telling the young Prince to clear away the sand because the Sphinx was choking on it. The Sphinx said to him that if he did this, he would become King of Egypt.

According to documentation the Sphinx was carved during the reign of pharaoh Khafra
c. 2558–2532 BC

Over time, approximately 1000 years, 50-65ft. of sand and debris covered the structure and the surrounding area. Plainly the Sphinx acted as a natural dam and the build-up of debris would be considered above average. This would indicate there was a large volume of surface sand-debris on the plateau.

Remember this is surface material and we still have to get down through any subsoil to reach bedrock for a solid foundation.

Which implies for them to prepare the foundation excavating a minimum of 65ft of debris to reach solid bedrock is a very conservative assessment. In fact it could have been as much as a hundred plus feet.

Excavation of the Foundations

The modern terrain of the Giza plateau where the pyramids stand would have been totally different before any of the pyramids were built.
It's standard practise on any building plot for the site to be cleared first. Bear in mind they would have dug down to approx. 65ft through the top soil (sand-debris) as well as through the subsoil down to the bedrock.

If the ancient Egyptians were actually more advanced and technically more able than us it's at this point in the construction process we believe they would have turned things on their head. The Egyptians did the complete opposite in preparing the foundations for the pyramids to any other building in history, modern or otherwise.

Whereas many buildings throughout history would have footings dug out which are in effect trenches in the ground which would be filled in with solid material back up to the original ground level to secure a solid foundation for the structure.
Or another technique is to dig out the footprint of the building through the terrain to a solid base. And the footprint of the building is in-filled with solid material up to the original ground level. In the case of the pyramids these techniques were not employed.

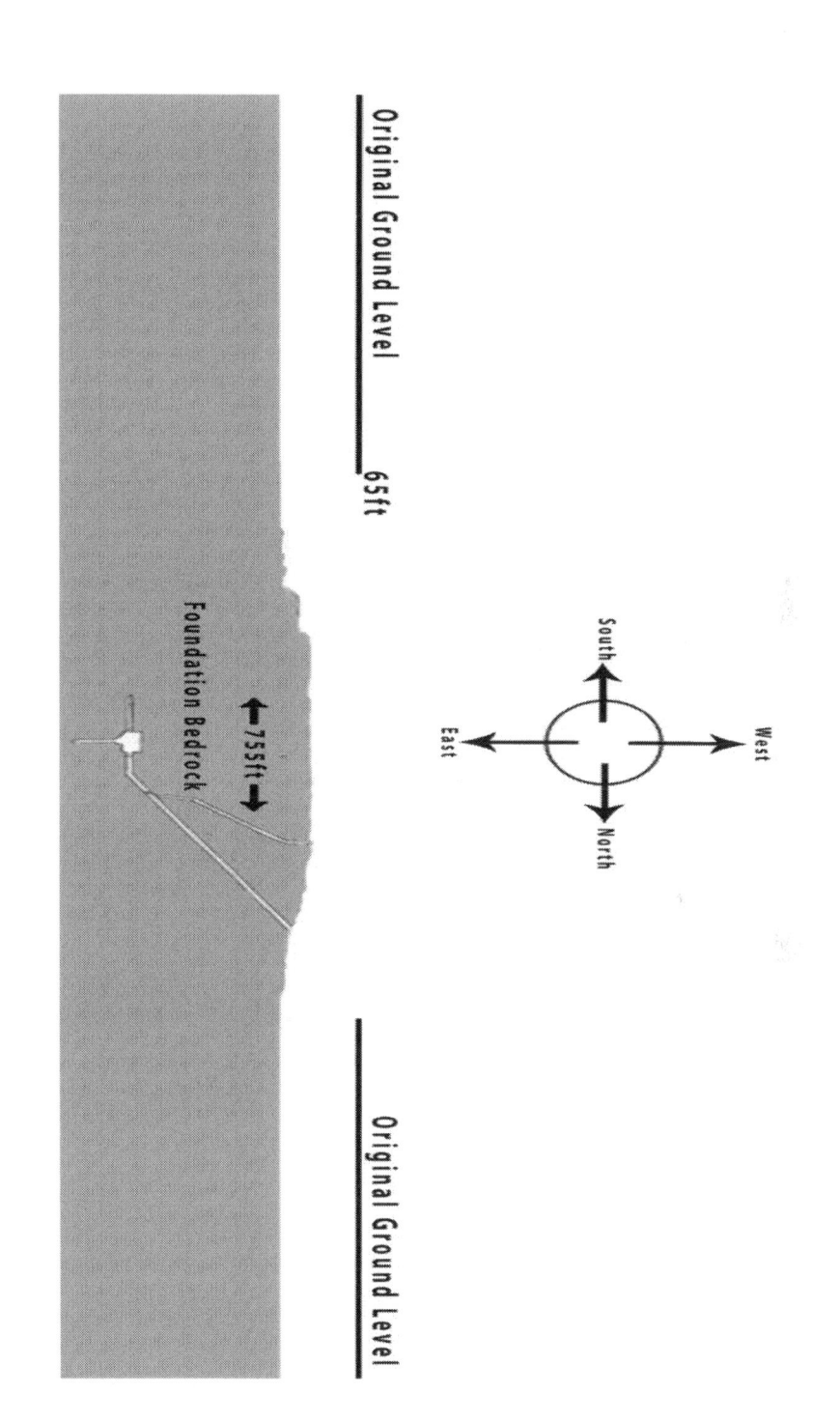

Normally when you view any building modern or otherwise you are unable to see any part of the foundations.

When in fact you look at the Great Pyramid apart from any wind swept surface debris on the Giza plateau today the foundations of the pyramid are clearly exposed indicating the obvious, that the first layer of the pyramid can clearly be seen by all. This is a very misleading fact in the analysis on how the pyramids were built.

This fact implies that the plateau was clear before building commenced. We do not perceive this to be the case. We conclude that one of the biggest oversights that many have made, when trying to decipher the building formula of the pyramids is that these structures are viewed with a similar mindset of other buildings. When in reality the pyramids are totally unique in their design.

With this in mind a unique approach would have to have been devised for the foundations. They would be unable to use conventional methods due to the sheer weight of the structure. To avoid any subsidence or collapse the Egyptians would have to build on a solid base.

So they had no option but to remove all surface material down to bedrock. In reality this could be perceived as a major obstacle but actually this was their saving grace, as this problem created the solution for the pyramids to be built to such great heights.

With logical reasoning it's plausible that one of the most important commodities in the construction of the Pyramids was actually the excavated waste.

Remember it was essential for the Egyptian builders to make use of time as well as all materials to their advantage.
They would not have cleared the entire plateau they would've only dug out an area slightly bigger than the footprint of the pyramid approx. 850ft square with a minimum depth of 65ft.
In fact a giant hole and when workers dug out the sand, debris and rubble to expose the bedrock foundation, the materials that were excavated would have been stockpiled on the upper plateau to be utilised later.

The open sides of the exposed area would need to be graduated back to avoid collapsing. This is standard practise in all excavations. This is the stage where things start to take a twist and we believe the ancient Egyptians would have utilised the gradient sides.

In fact what they would've had was four ramps tapering from the original ground level down to the foundation forming an embankment ramp on all four sides at a suitable angle to aid a speedy delivery of blocks.

Levelling the Foundation

It's been suggested that the foundation base was flooded to ascertain its level. Some believe that a wall was constructed on all four sides and then the foundation area was flooded.

The walls retained the water while levelling took place, very similar to a *giant swimming pool*, in fact 570025ft the equivalent to 42 Olympic swimming pools. This procedure is not conducive with the timeframe in hand.

Every working moment had to be utilised to its full potential. The more time spent on levelling, the less time there is to finish the construction. We've devised a simple solution to what appears a complex and arduous problem but first we have to clarify what the problem actually is.

The challenge is not just to determine the level of the foundation, it's to do so in a practical way that does not hinder the workforce, whereby the levelling is not jamming-up the overall build and cutting into the timetable. By using water in the manner described work cannot commence on the subterranean level.

Ideally they would need to start as soon as possible on the subterranean levels otherwise their task will become more demanding with each tier of the pyramid. Every part of the project has to work in unison and they could not permit any section of the build to create obstacles that would slow down or congest the overall process.

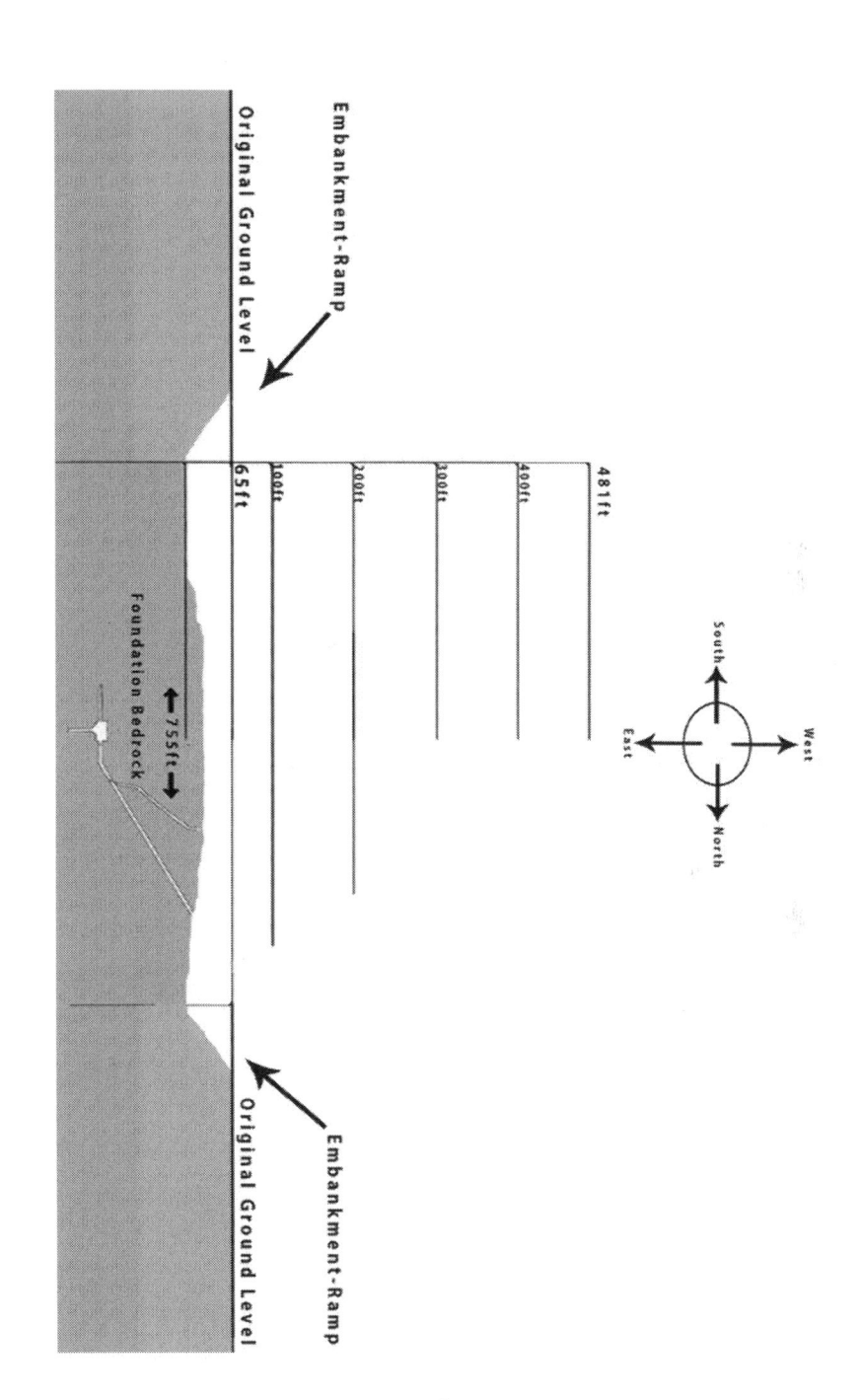

Our Solution to Levelling the Base

Determining the level of the base would've been a very easy obstacle to overcome.

In fact the ancient Egyptians would've held the solution in their hands every day, whenever they took a drink of water or wine.

Because all they required was a vessel of water and a long piece of string or rope, the equivalent of our spirit level today, as liquid always finds its own level. It's hard to comprehend this ancient civilisation can achieve such great feats as building the pyramids but are incapable of devising a simple levelling device.

Let us explain:

Logically speaking we know they made clay pots and were able to weave garments, rope etc. basic facts. We accept they were able to cut, carve and shape timber.

With that in mind we use a combination of these facts to establish the invention/use of the first equivalent of today's spirit level. These levelling instruments could easily be devised.

The vessel would be shaped to their necessary design and left on a level surface. A small hole would be made near the base and plugged. It would then be filled with a dye up to the required level left to settle and then the plug would be removed draining the dye.

The potter would make good the hole and then the vessel was hardened. Now 13 acres, 755ft. squared, is a vast area to level.

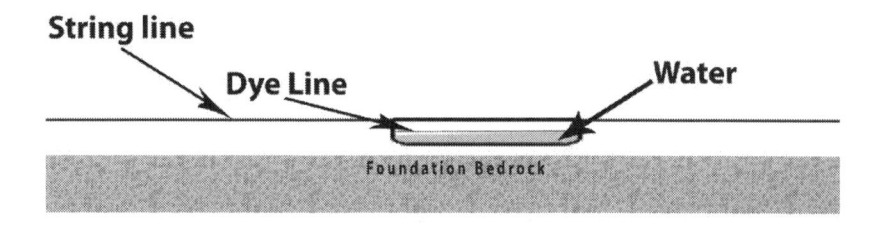

Reference points would have been made across the area of the foundation and string/rope would be stretched between 2 points whether they are 50 or 100ft. apart.

And with the vessel of water attached to the rope-string, however far off the dye line the water was would determine the level.

As these devices could so easily be tailor-made vast numbers would be available to the workmen. Yet at first glance these crude designs could be mistaken for simple pottery.

We believe that our explanation is far a simpler approach than flooding the equivalent of 13 acres. The foundation surface would have been levelled where necessary, any high spots chipped down, any low spots could have been filled with crushed granite-limestone etc. and compressed. It's worth mentioning that the entire foundation was not entirely level.

Above the subterranean entrance there is a protrusion in the foundation and not all corners are level with each other. Once the foundation was prepared the building of the pyramid can commence.

Now at this moment you would think that the surrounding terrain has been completely cleared giving the impression that the plateau is level with the bedrock.

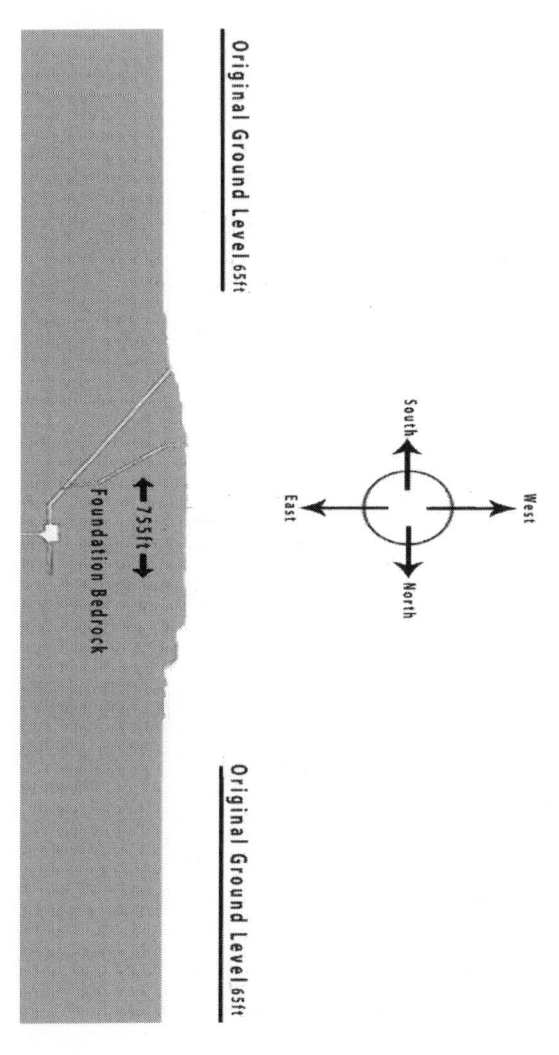

Outer Perimeter is Squared and Marked

Once the foundation was prepared and levelled, the outer perimeter of the structure would be marked out and squared before building commenced.

Logically speaking hundreds, if not thousands of men would be working on site at any given time. If anyone were to make a mistake with the alignment of the blocks without doubt this would have repercussions throughout the structure.

There were various methods that they could have used.

Examples:

Reference points could be marked or cut-out on the granite base to keep true alignment.

Another method possibly used was holes could've been cut into the granite base and sticks placed within the holes to act as reference points.

It's been common practise for centuries to use string lines as a reference to ensure alignment when building.

However in the case of the pyramids we believe that string lines, sticks or markings on the base would create more of a hindrance than a reference. As they would be an obstacle to the workers and if disturbed, or lost due to foot traffic and the large amount of blocks and materials arriving, everything would have to be re-aligned and re-marked again, losing precious time.

The Datum Wall

To ensure the building remained square the practical solution would be a perimeter wall to act as a solid Datum line approx. 13ft. (4mt) away from the base of the pyramid. The Datum wall would act as a reference point for building the outer boundary of the first layer.

This technique would speed up construction immensely due to the fact that any worker could reference the outer point of the perimeter at any given time.

There would be no chance of their reference point being lost or a string line being knocked etc. The benefit of this technique is that the hundreds of workers would not be waiting for engineers to pinpoint the precise position of each block.

Once the first layer was in situ the outer edge of the structure naturally becomes its own Datum line and continued throughout the build. Before the construction of the Datum wall the majority of the blocks for the first layer are positioned proportionately on the foundations working from the centre out.

Transportation of the Stone Blocks

Our opinion is that the blocks were transported on wooden sledges from the quarry and lowered down the embankment ramps and then transferred onto rollers, then transported to their designated point.

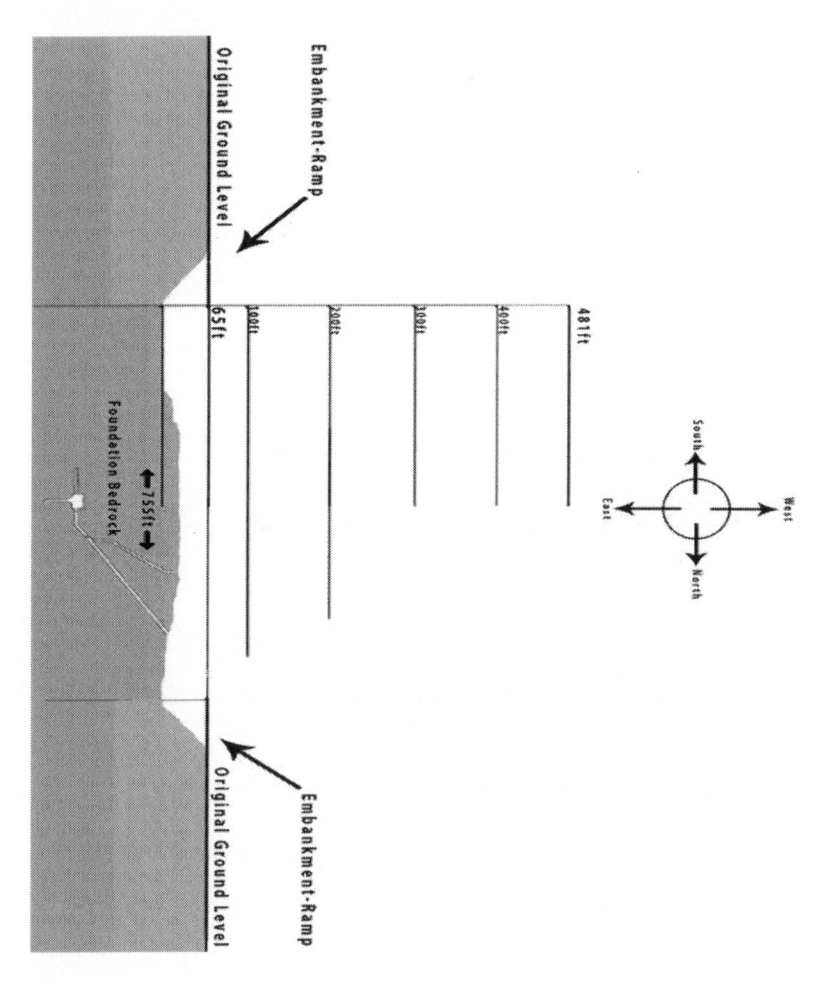

How the Embankment Ramps were Utilised

The majority of the largest blocks were used in the lower sections of the pyramid.

The embankment ramps allowed easy delivery downhill to the foundations.

Logically speaking why would the Egyptians clear the plateau of all surface debris prior to the build? If they had, after the first layer of the pyramid was in place, all subsequent layers would then have to be transported uphill.

Our method utilises the force of gravity to aid the transportation of many of the heaviest blocks increasing productivity to its maximum.

The embankment ramps are easily utilised by laying timbers on the ramps, similar to railway tracks, to aid the sledges in delivery of blocks downhill.

With this method realistically they could easily lower down 240 blocks per hour totalling 2880 blocks per day.

To accomplish this all they required were 10 teams on all 4 sides lowering 6 blocks per hour. (240 blocks per hour) A suitable surface working area on each embankment ramp of approx. 600 ft. allows each team a 60ft. working zone.

The possibility is they could have laid the largest surface area of the build, the first layer in less than 2 days.

We're not stating that they laid the first tier in 2 days. However, with our technique the possibility exists whereby if they could position and lay the blocks as fast as they arrive. It would have been realistically achievable to complete the first layer in 2 days or less.

The Datum Wall is then Erected

To accurately position the outer edges, two sides of the Datum wall are completed forming a 90 degree angle.

To ensure perfect alignment of the outer blocks we believe they would have used pieces of timber (Datum rule timbers) cut to the exact same length. One end lay against the Datum wall and the block is then placed tightly up against the other end of the Datum rule timber ensuring that each block is positioned correctly.

Whilst the other two opposite sides of the Datum wall are being erected workers are already laying blocks on the second tier at the original starting point. When the first layer is completed the Datum wall becomes obsolete.

Obviously they would have to leave an opening on one side of the Datum wall, as not to cause an obstruction for delivery of the remaining materials for the first layer.

Remember once the first layer was laid the outer edge naturally became the Datum line and continued as such throughout the build.

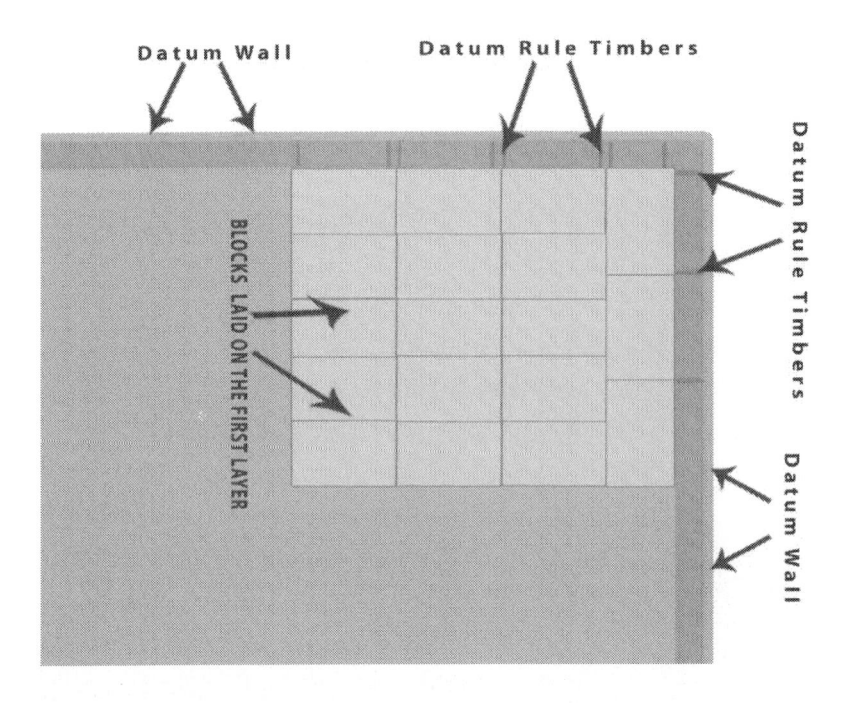

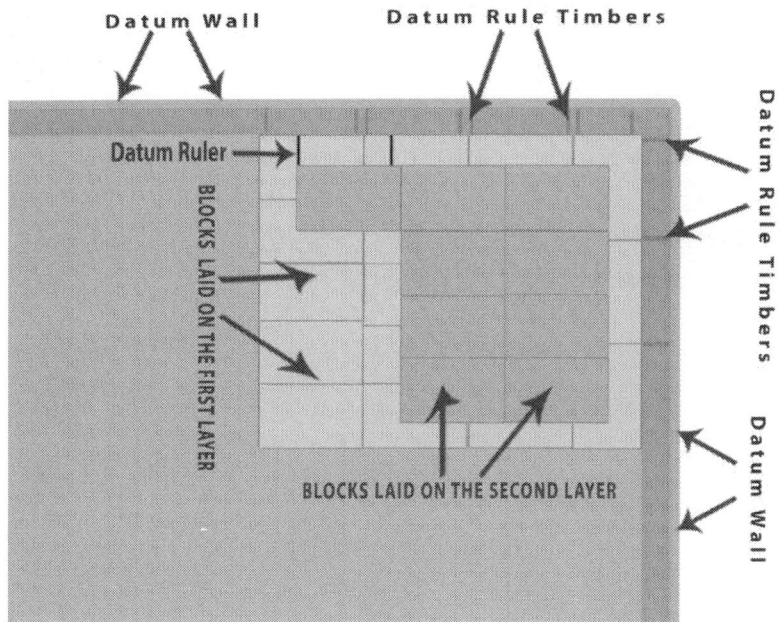

74

Datum Rulers

Once the outer edge of the first layer is in place datum rulers are used to position the outer edge of the second tier.
This process is used to position the outer edge of each and every tier throughout the build to ensure perfect alignment.

The significance of the Datum rulers was to ensure the precise positioning of each stone on the outer edge of the structure.

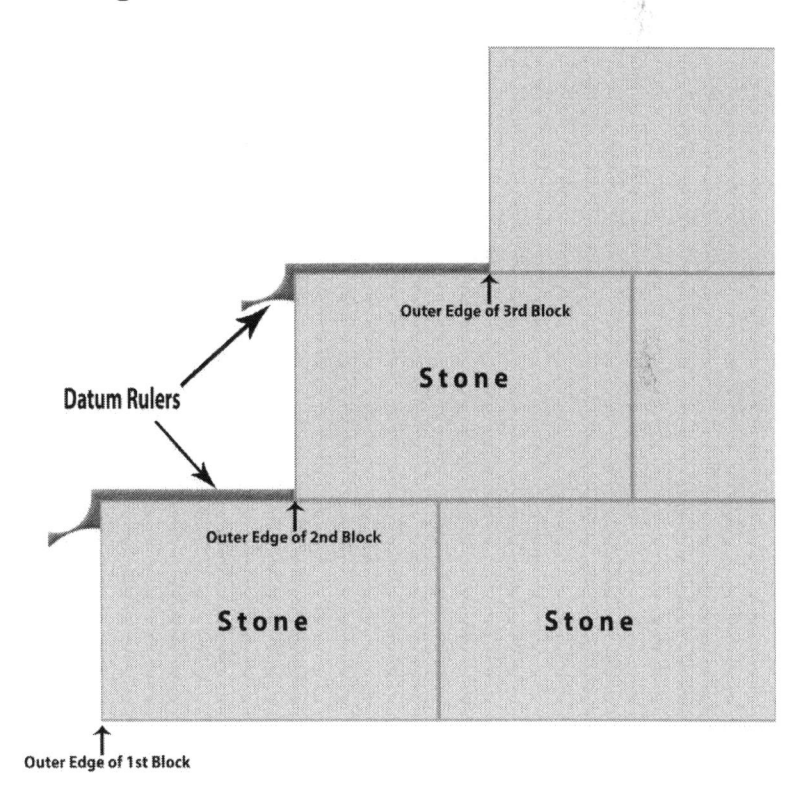

How the 52 Degree Angle was Maintained

The 21st century mind is perplexed! At what's be-lieved to be one of the most challenging factors on how the ancient Egyptians maintained the 52 degree angle throughout construction.

There have been many fantastic theories at how this 52 degree angle was achieved but with no simple solution to date. *Our solution* to this problem for the Egyptians to avoid any mistakes and to ensure a true angle was consistently adhered to is a simple yet effective method. The easiest way to overcome this challenge is to have a jig that they could effectively offer-up to the blocks and with very little skill could accurately determine at all times the angle was true.

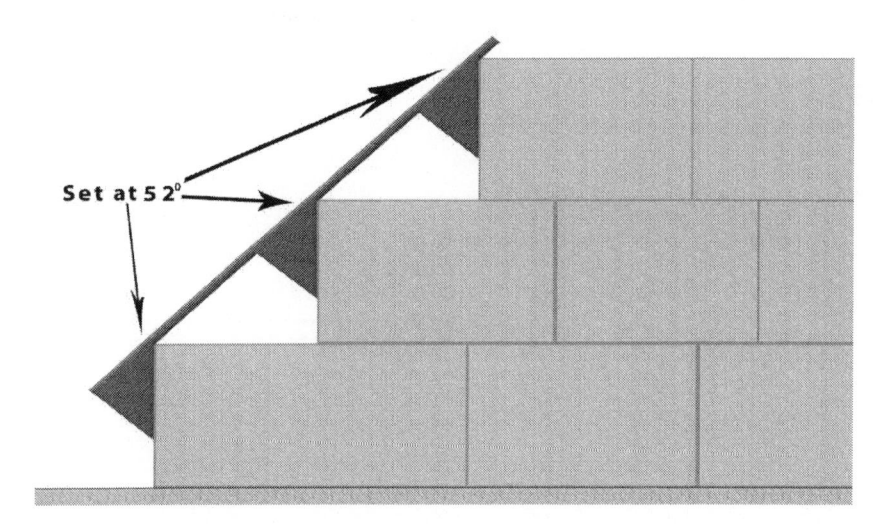

Set at 52°

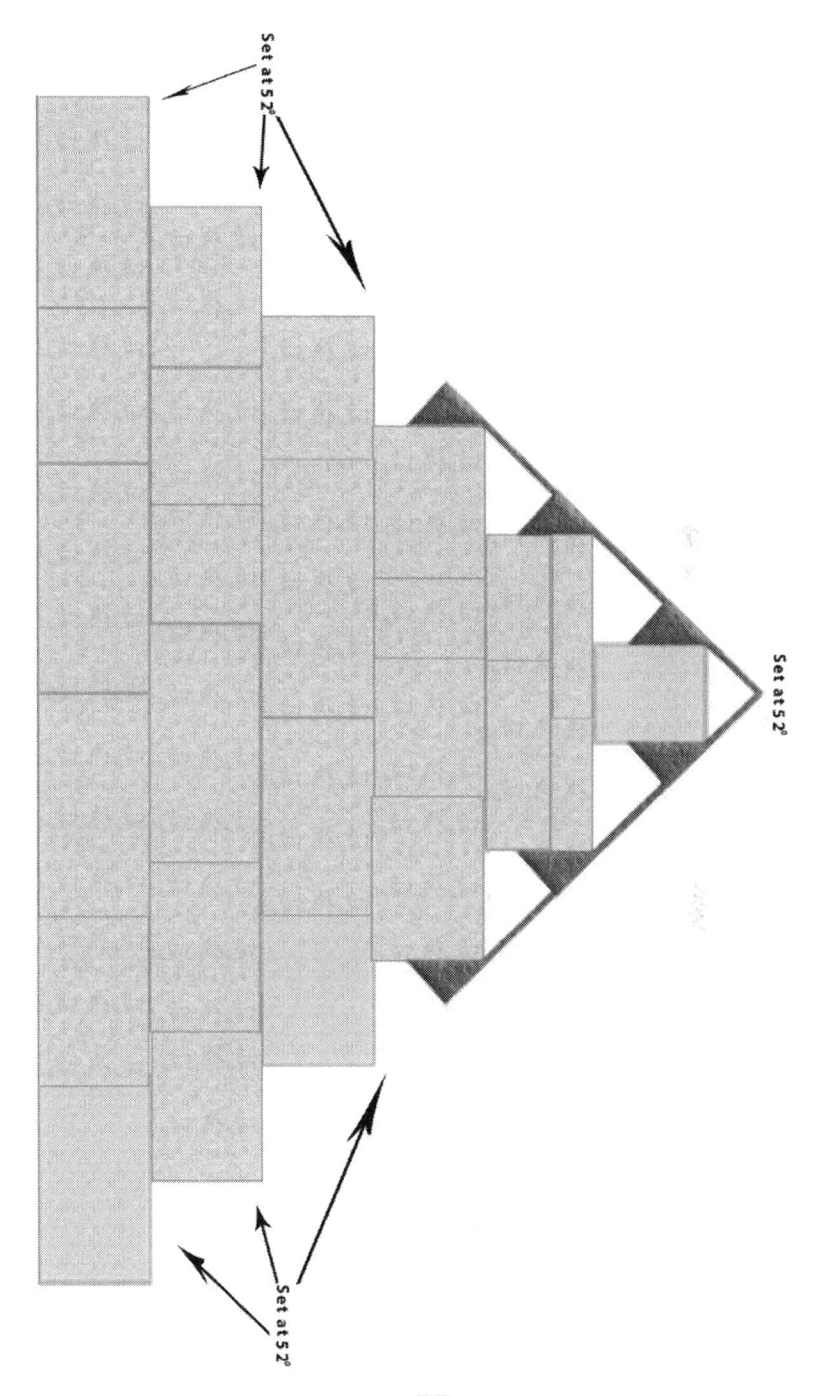

Set at 52°

Set at 52°

Set at 52°

How were the Blocks Levelled?

It is believed "A" frames with a 'plumb bob' were used for levelling the blocks even though this seems logical this method would be inconsistent considering the perfect unity and alignment of the existing structure.
As mentioned previously any defects would compound throughout the build.

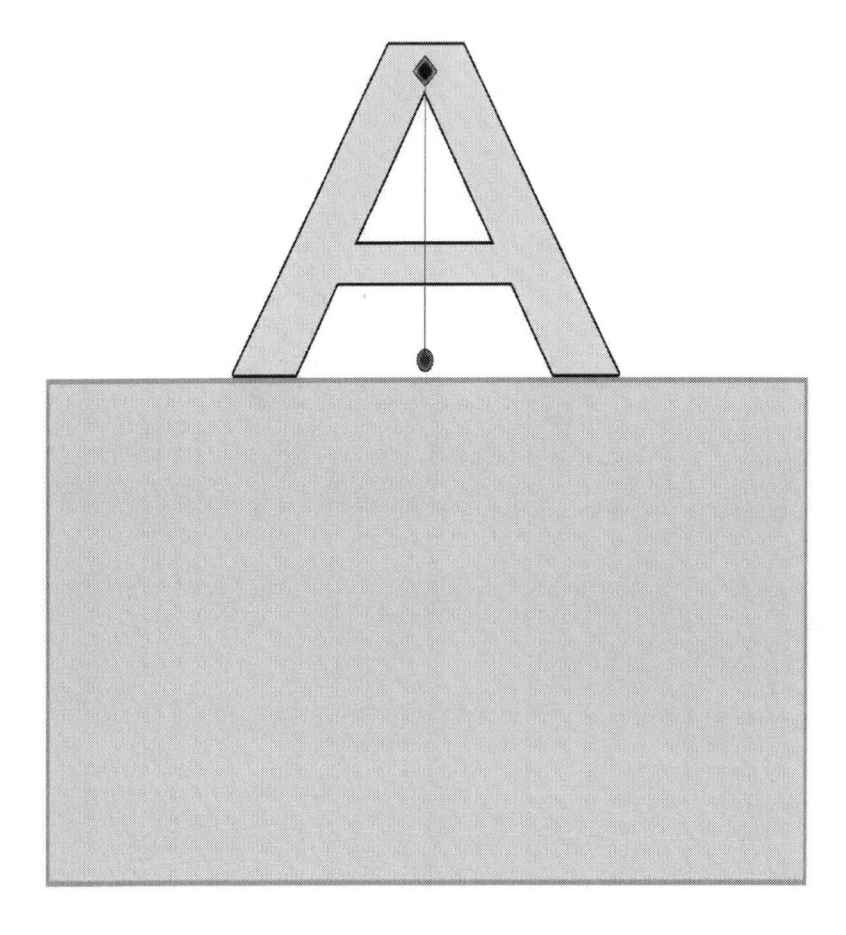

So we believe they would have used a more accurate method utilising a vessel of water (as previously explained) and a right-angle made of wood, similar to a carpenters square, combined with a plumb-bob to easily determine whether the stone was perfectly level and plumb.

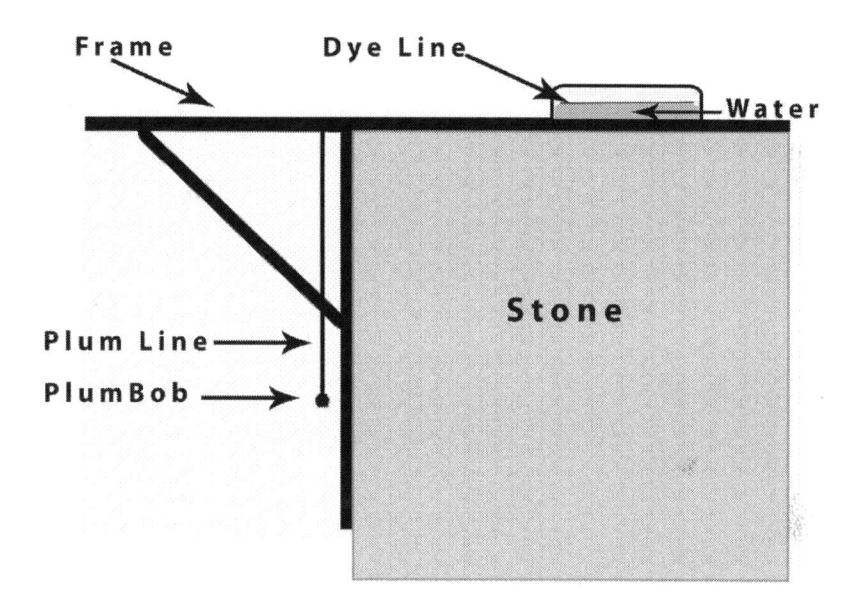

How the Blocks were Laid

Considering the size of the blocks used throughout the build you would imagine once placed they would not want to move them again. So it was necessary to ensure that initially each stone was laid and positioned perfectly.

To achieve this, a prepared levelled base to lay the stone upon was needed. Using some form of mortar sand or crushed limestone/granite etc. and a flat piece of wood as a rule to saw off any excess.

Checking that the prepared base was level, a vessel of water would be placed on a straight edge made from wood to ensure the bed was perfectly level.

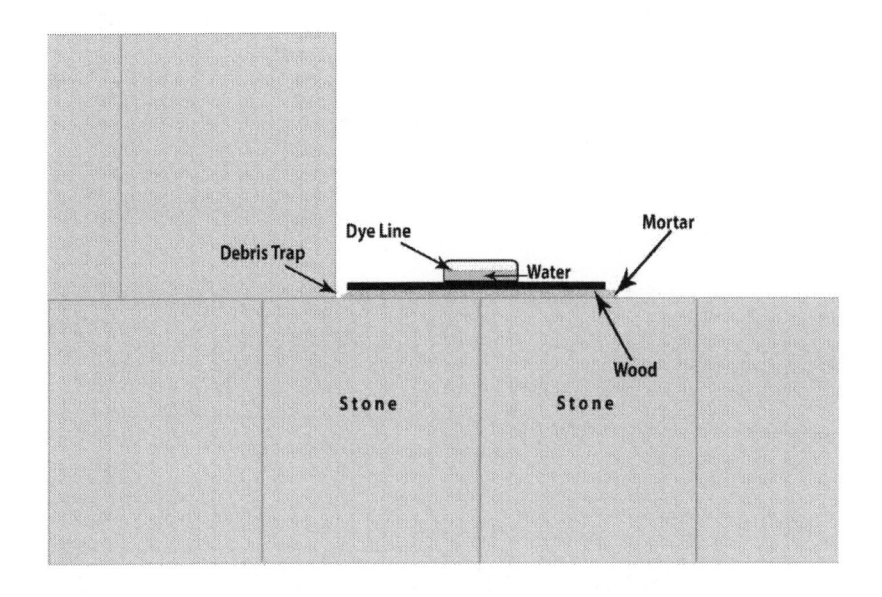

How they would have used the levelling device. A straight edged piece of timber would be laid on the mortar, the vessel placed on top of the timber then water poured up to the dye line.

If the water was on the dye line the area or would be perfectly level, if it was away from the line then they would know how far out the surface was.

The edges of the prepared base that adjoins any pre-placed blocks would have a "V'''" shape etched into the mortar to approximately 1-2ins in width. The necessity for this is, it acts as a debris trough ready for the stone to be placed.

It all sounds very straightforward and obvious, however, there are a few niggling questions that cast doubt.

For example: were the blocks simply rolled in and slotted into place? If so how were the rollers removed from the underside of the block? You may think they just simply pushed the stone off the rollers.

This would disturb the prepared base and if they pushed the stone tight to the front and side stone they would still be left with logically a couple of rollers underneath. Some may argue that sledges were used combined with 'A' frame hoists.

Large 'A' frame hoists could have been used as a hoisting mechanism to lift the stone from the rollers or the sledge.

This creates another problem as the ropes lifting the block would become an obstacle in between the joints never mind the time constraints involved in such a sluggish procedure. Another solution would be to lever the stone upwards whilst the rollers were removed.

This would not be the most practical way of placing the stone for a few reasons. Such a method would cause the level base to be pushed between the blocks that the stone was being placed against.

Some may argue there was no prepared layer and the stone was simply placed. What you must consider is that if the stone is forced into place to create a tight joint it's possible that some debris would definitely break off during such a procedure.

This debris would possibly fall and get trapped between the joints or underneath the block and could cause obstruction. If it were to fall beneath the stone, granted the debris may be crushed, but depending on the size of the debris it could cause the stone very marginally to be off level. If this continued with every stone placed the margin of error would compound with every layer.

Equating to every stone having to be redressed to ensure that it was plumb vertically and level horizontally. By having a layer of mortar, sand etc. and a small debris trough beneath the stone this would aid in absorbing any debris or margin of error.

The Technique used to Place the Blocks

It is assumed the blocks were transported on rollers which were of a similar size to the stone it was carrying.

The average size of the blocks was approx. 5x8x12ft. Working at the base level they used the larger blocks and the size of the stone decreased the higher the structure increased.

It is supposed that the stone was laid on the rollers 8ft across 5ft down and 12 ft. long, the rollers was presumed to be 8ft in length.

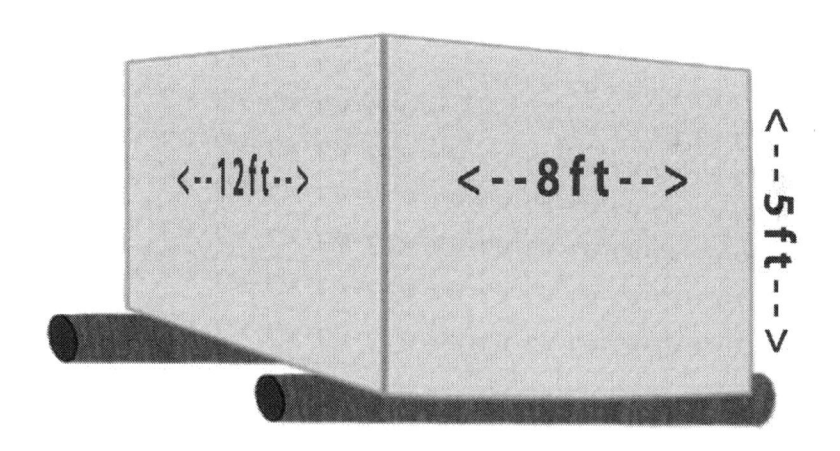

Our method is that the blocks were transported on the narrowest edge. The 5 ft. side was placed on the rollers, the rollers being approx. 5ft wide the stone being transported on the rollers 5ft wide 8ft high 12ft long.

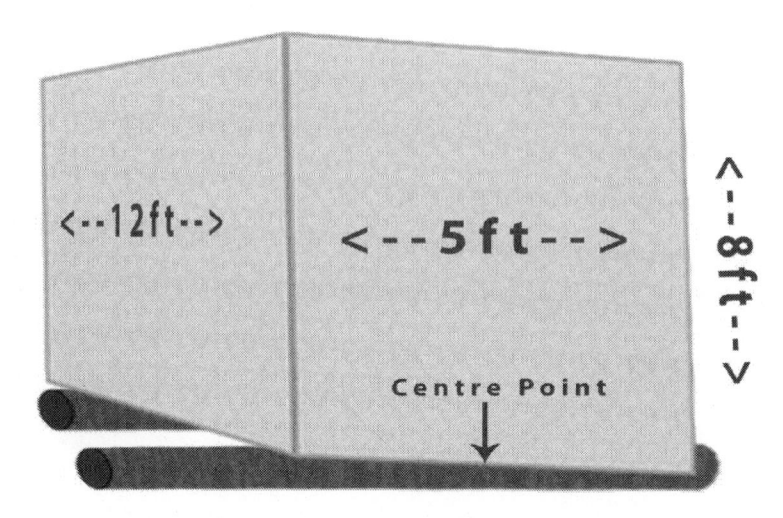

You may find this statement illogical because when you look at the structure the blocks are actually laid with the lowest side up.

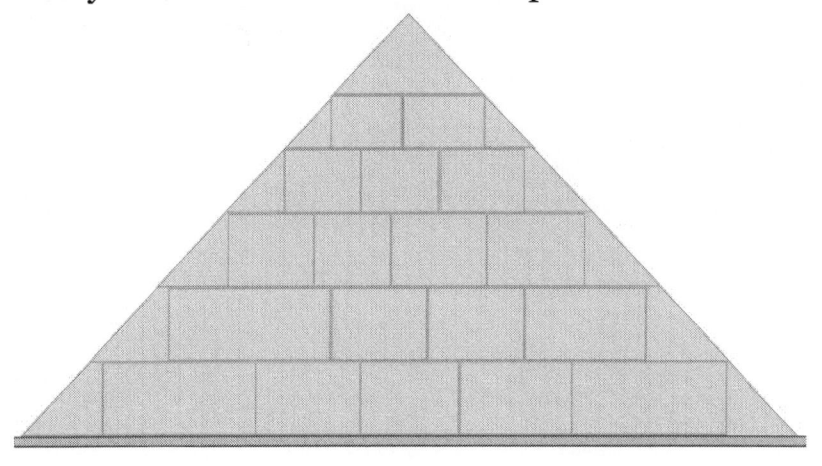

Our method alone cuts years off the building process as it enhances and speeds up productivity. Now we know our system contradicts previous theories, as it is believed that each stone was hoisted or brutishly pushed into place.

The consequence of such methods is that they not only bottleneck the build but demand a larger workforce. Stagnating the overall productivity and in addition delaying the whole construction.

However with our method the blocks own weight is harnessed by utilising the force of gravity enabling blocks, to be laid in mere seconds as fast as the blocks arrive they would be laid.

Placing the stone blocks on their 5ft side reduces the workforce needed along with the working area required during transportation, storage etc.

They had to lay 2.3 million blocks as quickly as humanly possible, they would not have used any technique that hindered or delayed the process. The longer it takes to lay each stone the longer it takes to complete the structure.

The main reason this technique would have been employed is because they could harness gravity utilising the blocks own weight when positioning, eliminating any unnecessary type of lifting devices. The stone's own weight would also be used to finish dressing the inside edges of its face and the outside edges of the adjoining blocks.

It was more advantageous for the blocks to arrive edge down on 5 ft. rollers When it is within a few feet of its final destination longer rollers would be necessary, approximately 4 times the width of the stone. The longer rollers would be positioned beneath the block just past the centre point.

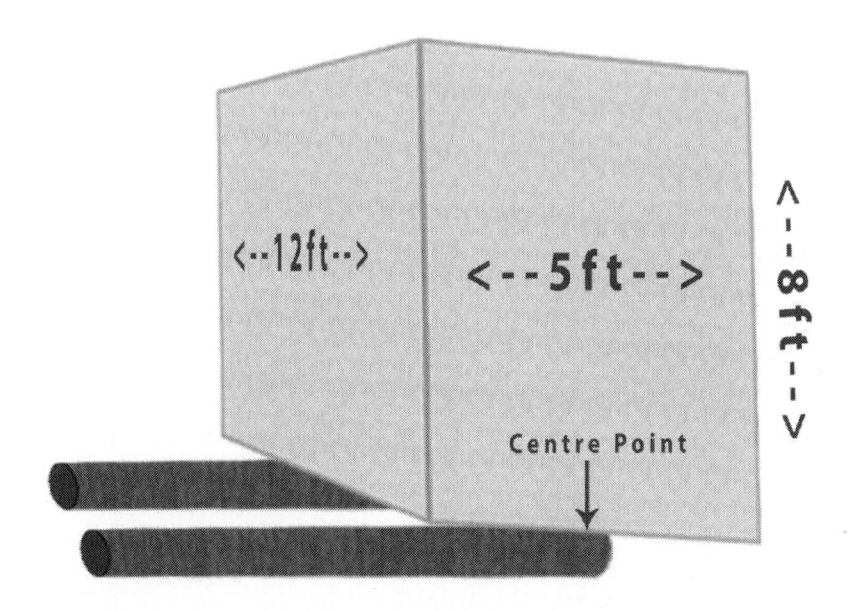

The stone would be rolled approximately its own width away from its final destination. The longer rollers would then act as levers to aid a precision placement of the stone.

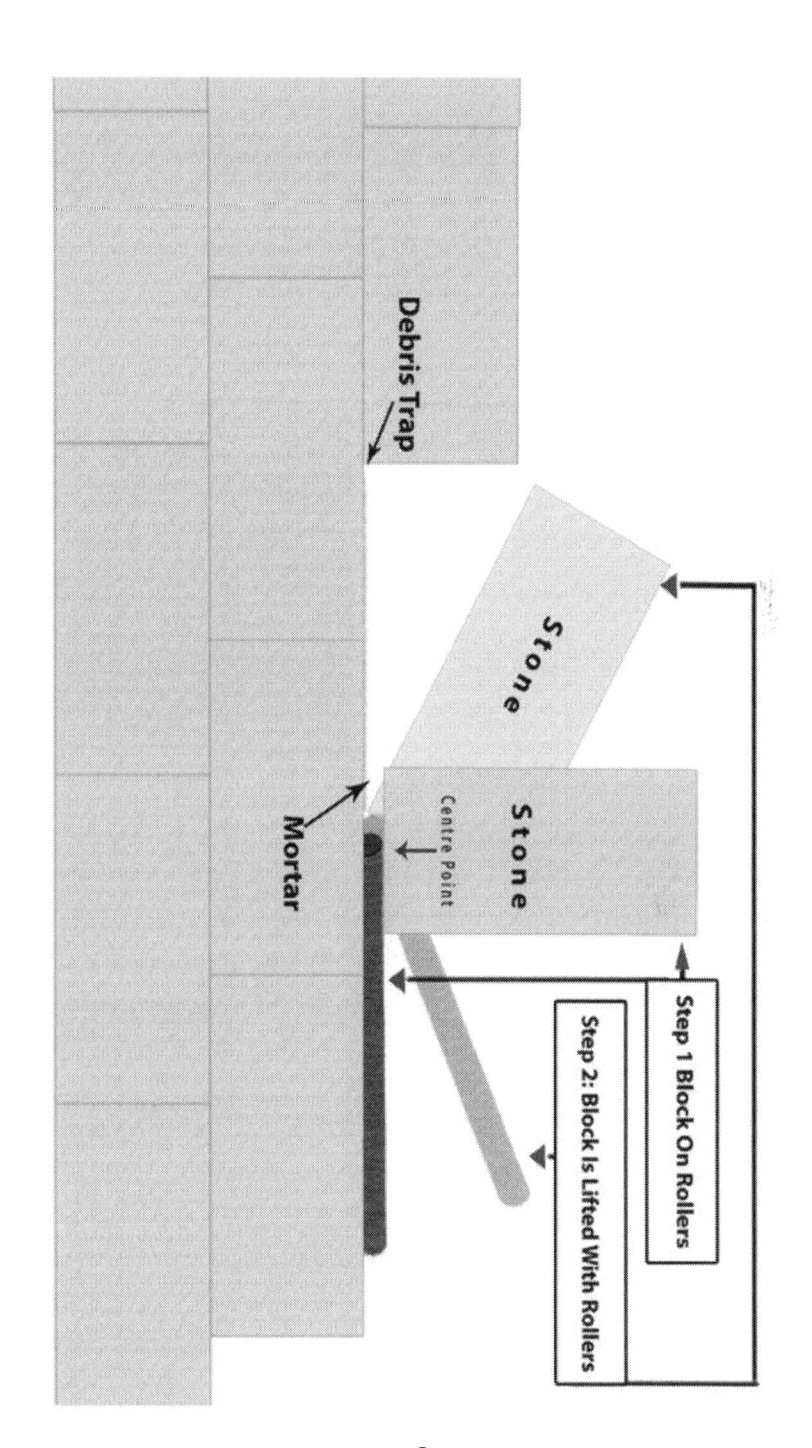

The Mechanics

The rollers are used as levers combined with physical strength. When the stone pivots a downward motion is applied to the rollers/levers with wedges underneath.
They would lever the stone precisely into place brushing down the face and edge of the opposing blocks it's being laid against, knocking off any imperfections during the movement. This loose debris falls beneath the stone into the debris trap.

As long as the stone was aligned correctly before it was tipped this method is very achievable rather than pushing or lifting the stone into place. Our method increases productivity and reduces the workload and labour force required overall reducing the time of the build by years.
Employing our method many blocks could be placed simultaneously whereas using a form of hoist etc. as previously documented, for positioning every stone would bottleneck and slowdown the building process.

Our technique can be applied even to the largest blocks. The measurement 5x8x12ft is the average, yet some blocks were much larger the majority of which were used in the lower sections of the pyramid. The higher the pyramid reached the smaller the blocks became.

Structure Takes Shape

Blocks were continually delivered down the embankment ramps from all 4 sides onto each tier utilising the force of gravity up to the original ground level of approx. 65ft (off the bedrock). The main entrance, passageways and chambers etc. were constructed within the structure throughout each tier continuing up to one layer above the original ground level.

At this stage they would have laid approximately 33% of the materials needed for the entire construction.

As each tier is completed the sides of the embankment ramps are raised level with the finished tiers.

The transportation of material onto the largest sections of the build was all downhill, apart from the layer above the original ground level, which reduced the time needed dramatically along with the number of workers required because gravity was working for them rather than against them.

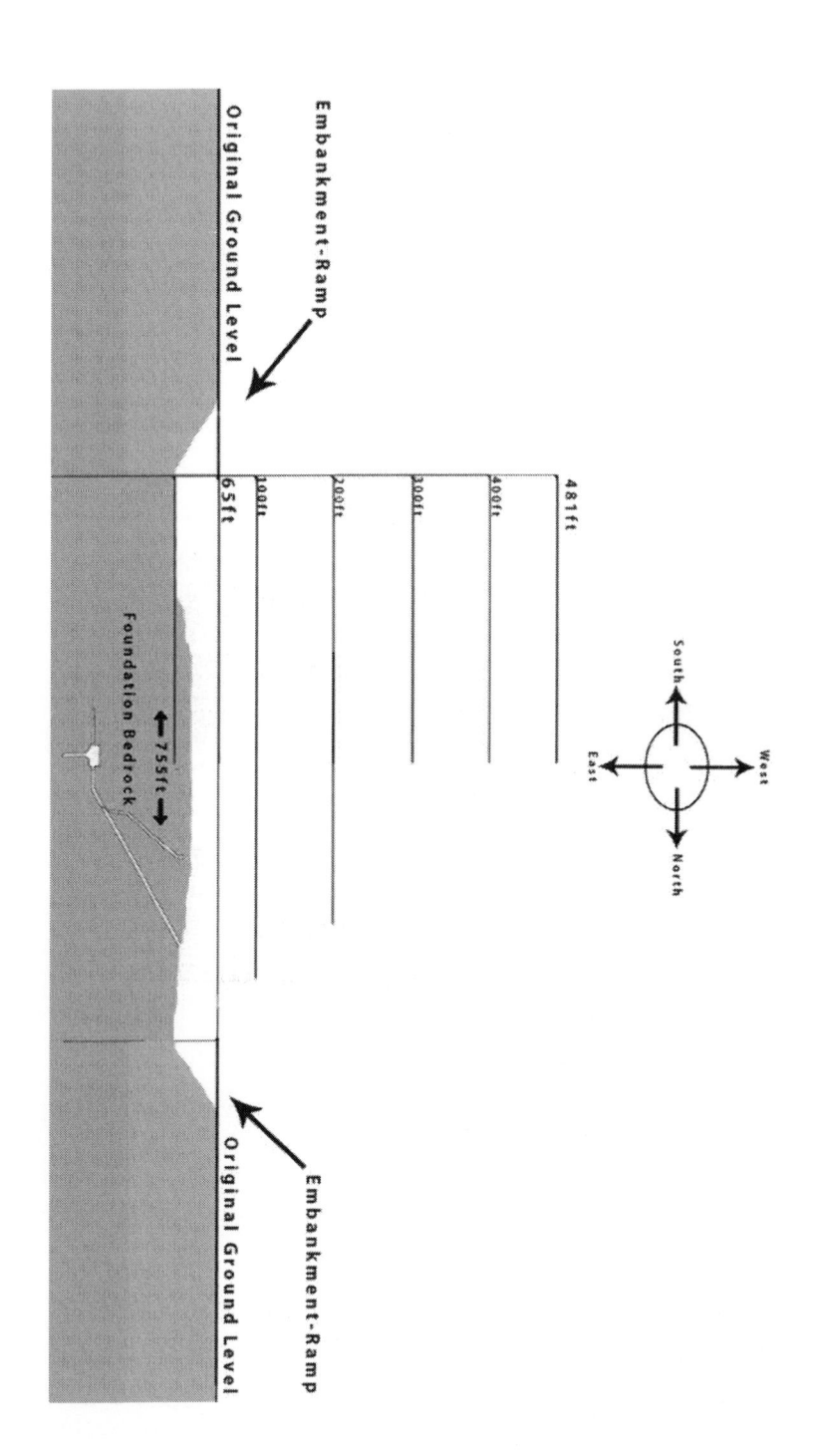

90

Giant Obstacle

At this crucial moment gravity will now begin to take its toll and the structure becomes the obstacle of the build. Plainly speaking they would be building a pyramid in their path.

The waste material that was originally excavated to expose the bedrock was stockpiled on all four sides of the plateau and would be used to raise the original ground level. In fact burying the pyramid as each layer is completed, grading back as necessary on all four sides to a gradient that enhances the delivery process.

By raising the ground level on each side and tapering back away from the pyramid they would've in fact created a ramp on all four sides allowing speedy transportation of the materials uphill.

Unlike any previous method to date with our technique, there would be no limited width restrictions on the ramps slowing down delivery of blocks or materials.

Enabling them to build the pyramid as fast as humanly possible. In fact they would have the equivalent of an overall working area on the ramps of approx. 2200ft - 550ft per ramp. The width of the ramps slightly narrowing as each tier is completed. Timbers were laid on the raised ground level, similar to railway tracks, to allow for the transportation of the blocks on wooden sledges.

As each tier was laid the voids were created for the inner passageways. The same applies to the inner chambers along with the Grand Gallery. All would've been constructed as their appropriate levels took shape. The Great Pyramid is unique when compared to other pyramids because of its internal layout.

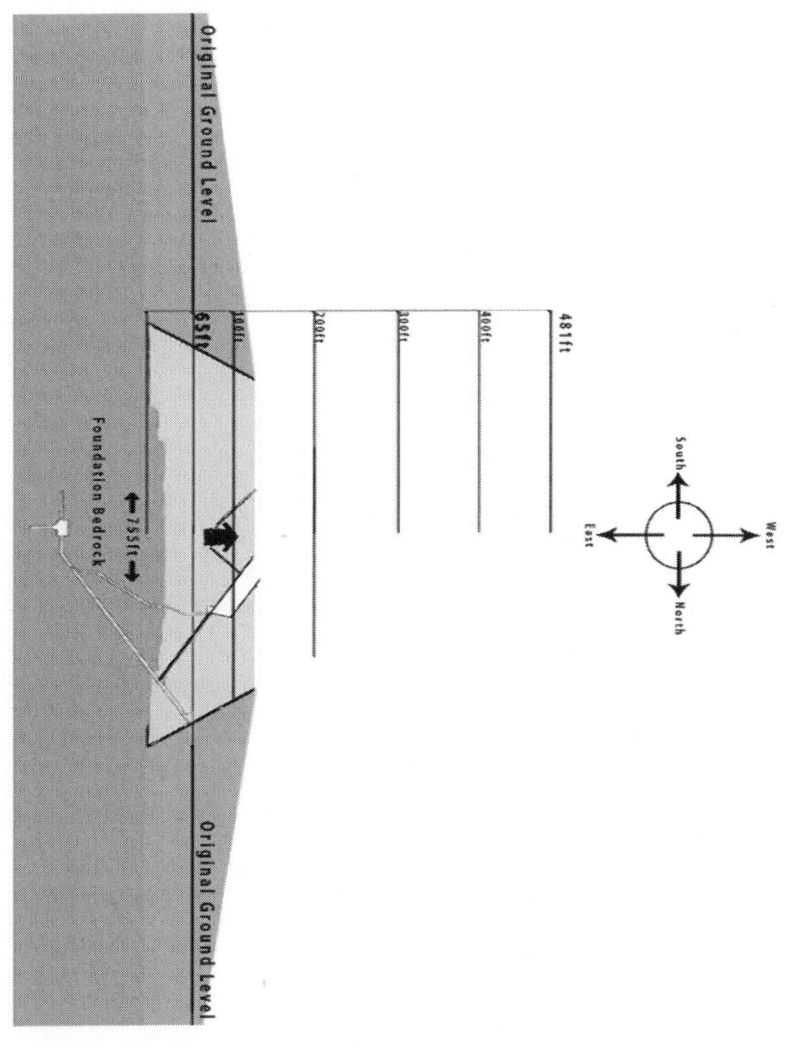

The Queens Chamber

The Queens Chamber is 18ft 10in by 17 feet 2 inches, 15 feet high. Although known as the Queen's Chamber, there is no evidence that any queen was buried here.

In the north and south walls there are vents approx. 8in sq. which do not continue to the outer surface of the pyramid they are capped off approx. at the 55th tier.

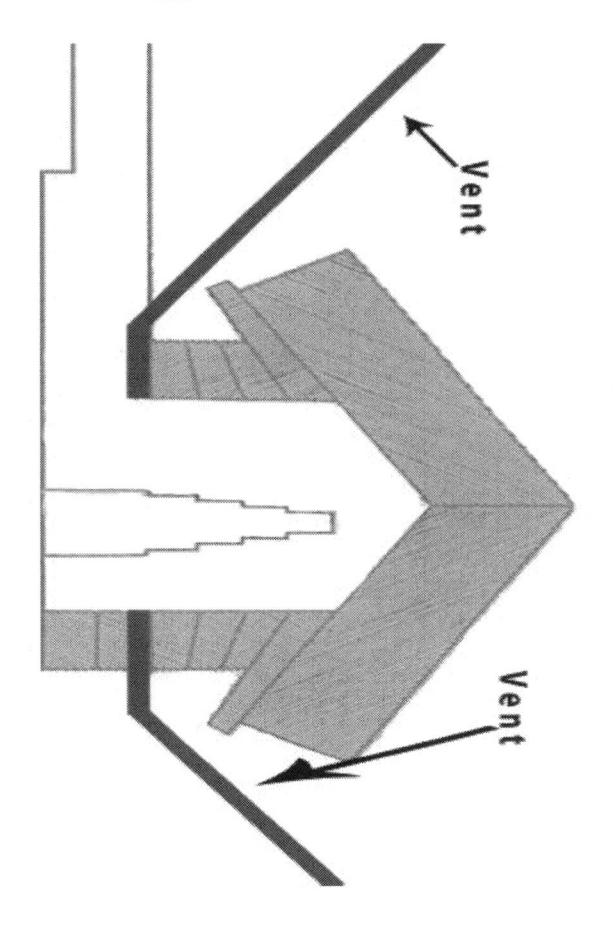

The Kings Chamber

The King's Chamber houses a granite sarcophagus, and is an extraordinary Chamber lined with rose granite and is situated at the 50th level approx. 141ft. above the foundation. It is 34.4ft long from east to west and 17.17ft wide from north to south and has a flat ceiling and the height of the Chamber is 19.6ft.

The two vents in the Kings Chamber are in the north and south walls approx. 3.6ft of the floor, each of these vents ascends through the structure to the outer surface unlike the vents in the Queen's Chamber.

Above the ceiling of the Kings Chamber there are 5 compartments known as the Relieving Chambers believed to be stress bearing Chambers to disperse the weight of the pyramid from above.

The granite used to construct this Chamber as well as the Relieving Chambers are documented to be some of the heaviest blocks in the entire pyramid.

The large granite blocks used in the construction of the Relieving Chambers are believed to be in excess of 40-50 tons in weight possibly as much as 80 tons.

Each beam is approx. 6.6ft thick and 26ft long, a combined total weight of around 400 tons.

Outside the Kings Chamber is the Anti-Chamber that housed the portcullis blocks which were used to block the entrance to the King's Chamber. This leads onto the Grand Gallery which is on a downward slope.

Grand Gallery

The Grand Gallery is 28ft high and 153ft long. The width is 7.5 ft. the walls of the Grand Gallery taper in marginally with each level of stone.

At ceiling level the overall width is 3.4ft at floor level there are 54 slots 27 on each side. There are also a variety of slots/holes cut in the walls. The floor slopes downward and in the centre sits a gutter.

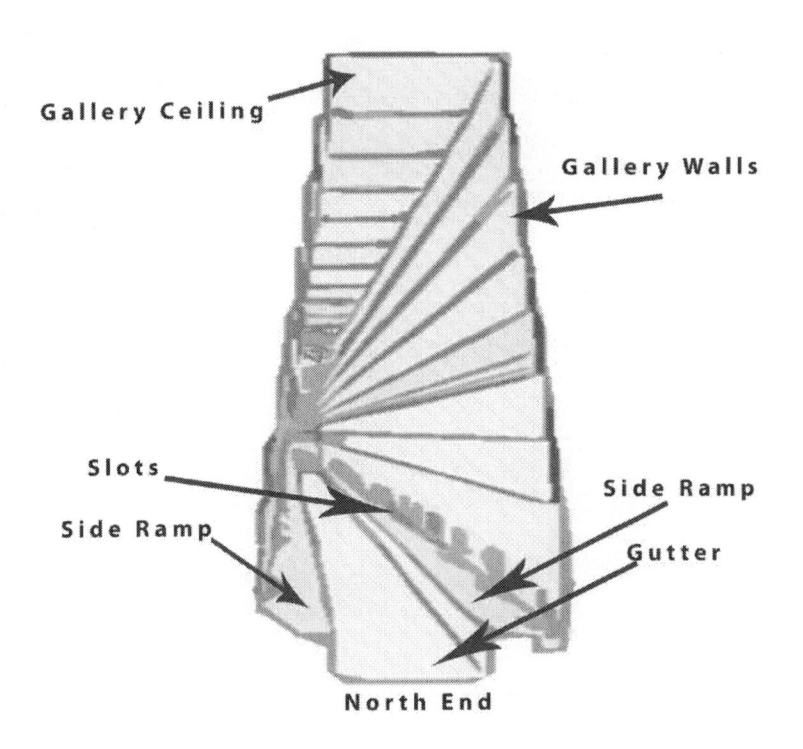

The Great Pyramid is believed to be the only pyramid to date that houses such Chambers or Gallery.

There have been many theories over the centuries that have tried to define the function of the Grand Gallery.

We consider that the sole purpose of the Grand Gallery was to aid in the construction of the King's Chamber.

One of the most difficult sections within the structure, we perceive, would be positioning the apex roof at the top of the stress relieving compartments above the King's Chamber.

By operating a configuration of counter-weights, within the Grand Gallery, they were able to lift and manoeuvre the heavy parts of the apex by controlling the counter weights to position simultaneously two of the giant granite apexes at a time, precisely into place.

90% Completed within 29 Months

90% of the structure was completed within 29 months. One of the tell-tale signs that support our method is the four vents within the structure. The two vents ascending from the Queen's Chamber and the two from the Kings Chamber. To date the Great Pyramid is the only pyramid documented to house such vents.

There is a great deal of conjecture surrounding these. It's believed they were not designed for ventilation as adequate air would flow through the main entrance to sustain the workforce working inside the pyramid.

This has led many to conclude that they're for religious purposes and act as spiritual ascending shafts.

Our analysis is the vents played a crucial part during the construction because the pyramid was being buried as each tier was completed. And the vents were necessary to supply ventilation for the workforce working on the internal parts of the structure due to the main entrance being buried underground.

It's illogical to accept that the ancient Egyptians spent their time and effort to incorporate the shafts into the build if they did not serve a purpose. As mentioned previously, time was of the essence and all parts of the project would have to work in unison.

We determined they continued burying the pyramid up until the vents of the Kings Chamber exited the structure on the north and south sides. Approx. 260ft. from the bedrock foundations in fact 195ft. above the original ground level.

Subsequently approx.90% (2,070,000) of the total number of blocks would be in place. We conclude they achieved this height realistically in a timeframe of 29 months, leaving the remaining 10% (230,000 blocks) which was accomplished in 23 months.

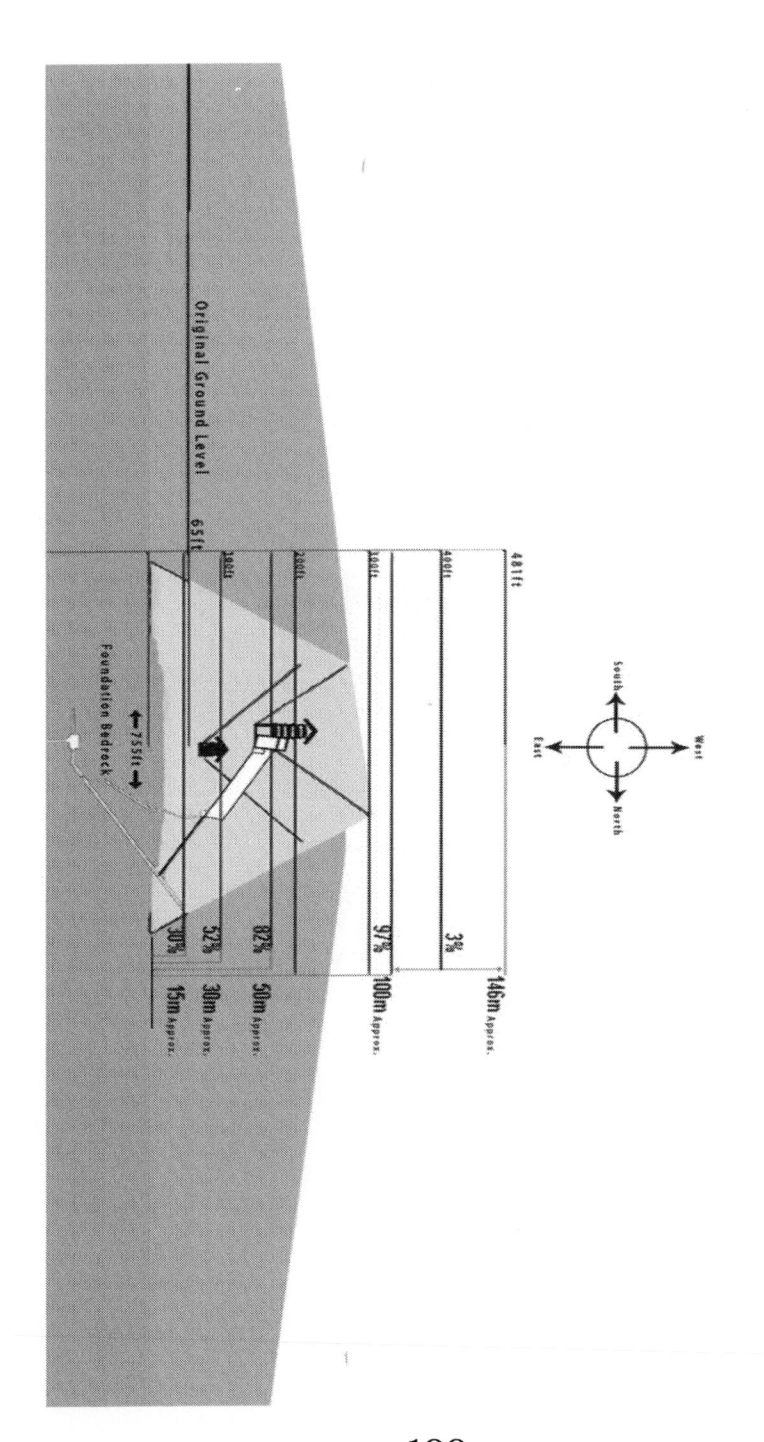

To continue this process once the vents exited the structure would be impractical as the vents from the King's Chamber would become blocked. Therefore they would have to remove the materials from the north side to reveal the entrance. The debris removed from the north side would have been transferred to build up the ground level on the east and west sides this process continuing until they reached the summit.

Completing the structure in 4 years and 4 months, however, if they transferred the dirt from the north side and placed it on the east or west side the timeframe would have been much longer. As they would only have been able to transport the remainder of the materials on one side subsequently being restricted slowing down the overall process and completion would've taken longer 6 years and 3 months.

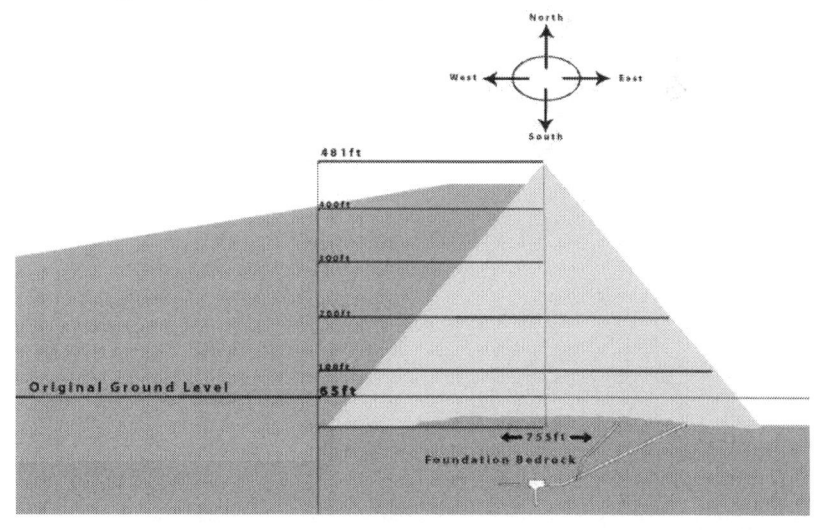

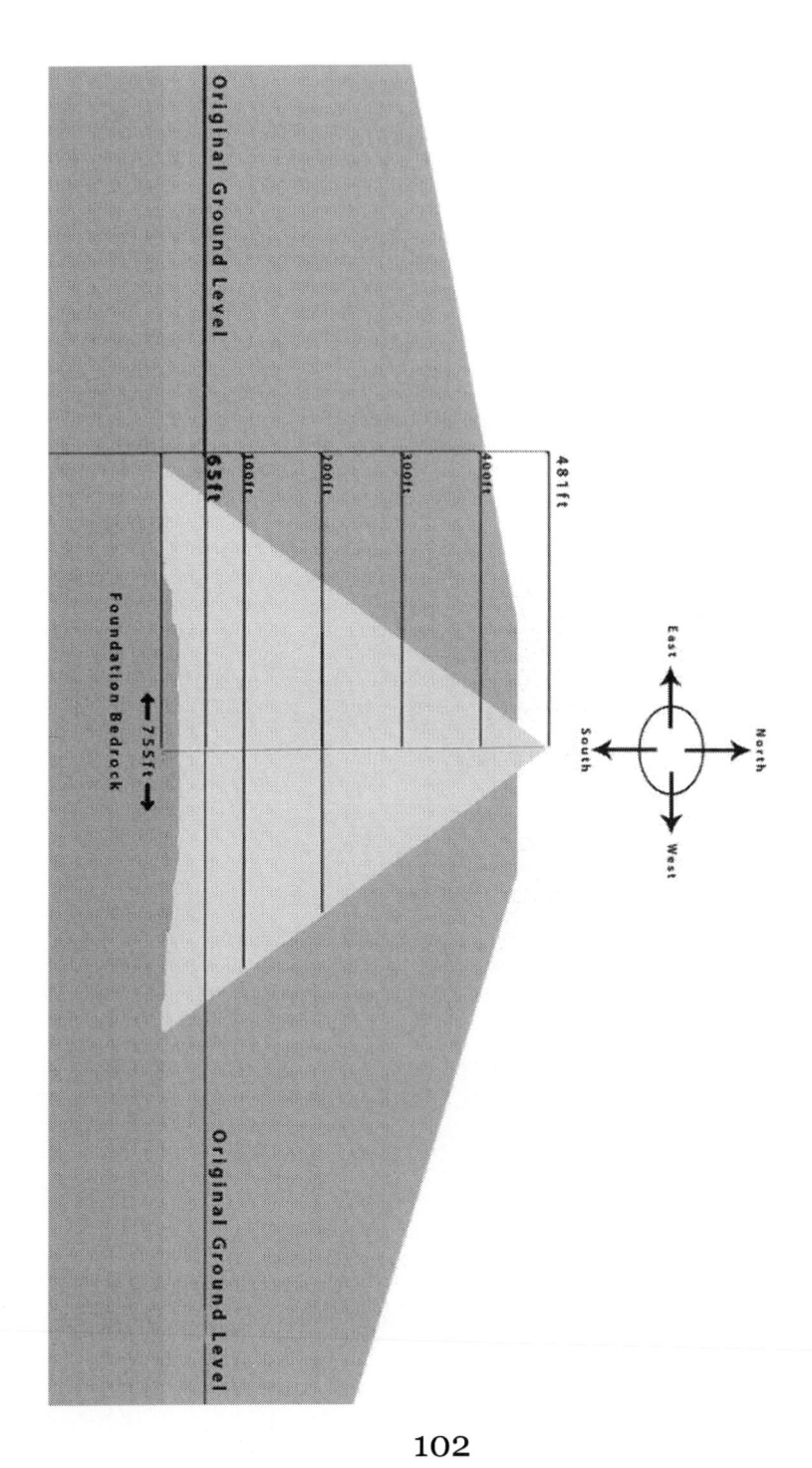

Previous Theories Prove Impractical

The long ramp theory once believed the solution to the construction of the pyramid lost its credibility. As a specially constructed stone ramp would prove too impractical and time consuming to erect and would be more of an achievement than building the Great Pyramid.

As the ramp would be over 1 mile in length, 475ft high, with a footprint of 755ft

tapering up to approx. 15ft wide.

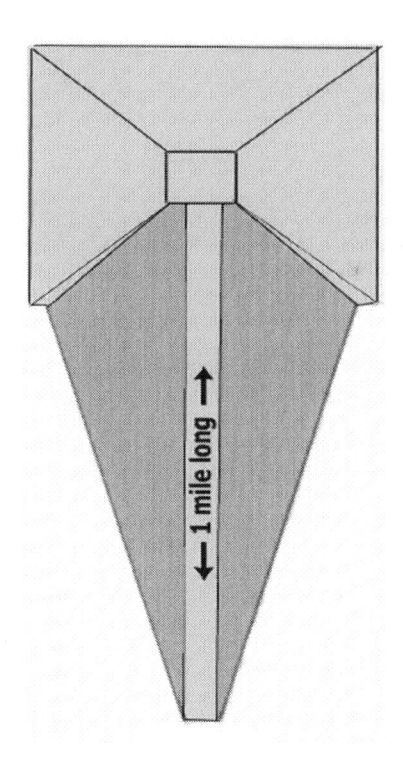

1 mile long

Long Ramp

If any of the documented ramp, hoist or winch theories etc. to date, were utilised the pyramid would not have realised its purpose in a practical timeframe, because the labour force would have been restricted.

For example with an internal or external spiral ramp the width limits the number of teams transporting blocks and slowing down the whole overall process.

The overall time of 2m 16sec per block during a 20 year period is a consequence from such theories.

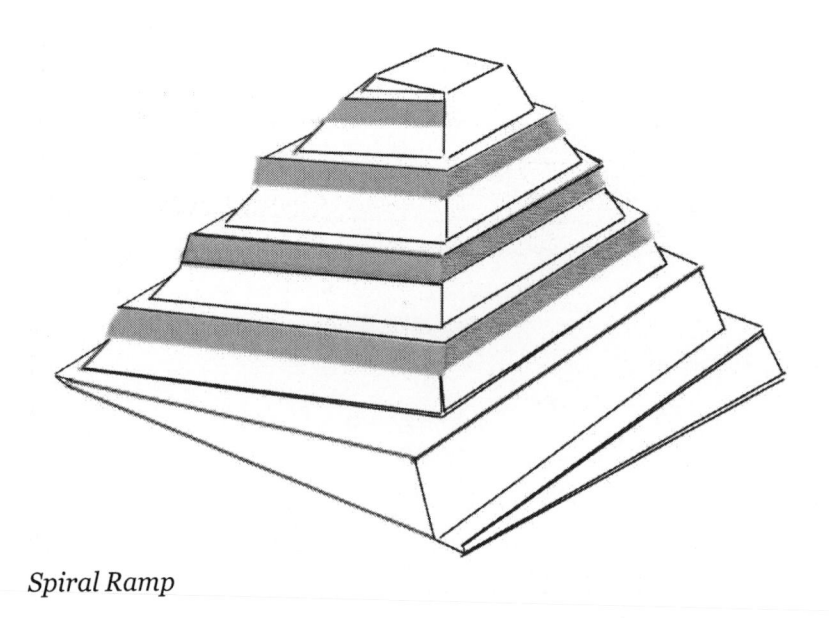

Spiral Ramp

Our solution

The pyramid acts as a natural dam and any excavated materials were effectively not to build a ramp but in fact to raise the ground level around the pyramid and tapering it out to a gradient that was acceptable for the prompt delivery of blocks and materials.

Ultimately regardless of the height of the structure the blocks never have to leave the ground. Using our method no skill was needed to raise the ground level and the workforce and materials to achieve such a task would easily be sourced. The sheer volume of dirt is positioned to retain itself to allow materials transported throughout each level.

This may seem somewhat elaborate but considering the landscape known as the Giza Plateau where the Khufu Pyramid stands would have looked very different in the 4th dynasty than today, as the ground level of the Giza plateau in the 21st century is much lower than 4500 years ago.

The surface area would have contained thousands of tons of materials that were excavated prior to any construction, a task they would have undertaken either way.

All we have simply done is use this as an advantage and not discarded it and the fact that the nearby surrounding terrain held an unlimited source of materials.

Taking into account that the higher the structure grew the blocks generally were not only smaller and lighter but a lot less were required. It is entirely possible that the remainder of the structure could have been honeycombed leaving voids between some of the internal blocks to reduce the weight over the King's Chamber reducing the overall amount of blocks needed to complete the structure.

Another fact to take into account is with satellite technology modern scientists have discovered many other pyramids buried beneath the earth. It leaves you with the question were they buried naturally overtime or were they buried as they were built in fact underground tombs?

In the case of the pyramids/tombs of Egypt we perceive looking back through time these great monuments are there to be seen by all.

Many of the discoveries in Egypt have been unearthed. Who is to say that the ancient Egyptians cleared all the sub-terrain entirely because you have to ask the question why is the entrance to the Great Pyramid 55ft above ground level?

Was this a design specification or was it in fact that after any wind swept surface debris away, 55ft was the original natural ground level?

The sole purpose of the pyramid creates the obvious question; how did they get the Pharaohs body 55ft up to the pyramids entrance?

They could have built a ramp to facilitate his delivery to his tomb because you couldn't imagine them hauling his body up the side of the pyramid. This was their leader, their Pharaoh soon to be their God. The question does create pause for thought......

SUMMARY

Over 4 millennia numerous adventurers and academics have attempted to unravel the genius of the ancient Egyptians. This man-made 7th wonder of the world often reminds us how inferior we are. The Great Pyramid of Giza is enveloped in a stirring awe of intelligence, mystery and it's easy to become entwined within its mystique.

We're sure you've witnessed magicians performing an illusion that captures your attention, your imagination, but once you've been given insight into the techniques that surround the illusion it can sometimes lose its value, we suppose that's just human nature.

However, you could never dismiss the genius of the ancient Egyptians. The driving force of the ancient Egyptians was their religious beliefs which motivated them to complete this massive tomb for their Pharaoh in a timeframe of less than 7 years to ensure his final resting place

So were the ancient Egyptians actually more advanced than us today? Did aliens really build the Pyramids? Or maybe it's just that within our modern society our minds are often so cluttered that we sometimes cannot see the 'wood for the trees'.

Yet the Egyptians of that era didn't have that luxury, they had more urgent matters to deal with and the building of the Great Pyramid of Giza was at the top of their agenda.

You may feel that building this great monument in a period of less than 7 years somewhat controversial. However, Pharaoh Khufu along with his subjects expected his final resting place to be prepared in time. Consequently from the architect to the water carrier and throughout the chain of command all had to have precision thinking and discipline to enable the 7 year project to be completed on time.

We hope you have enjoyed the experience in sharing our views and ideas on this sensitive yet intriguing mystery and we trust you will find our next book equally fascinating 'Evolution or God?'

This will offer an in-depth analysis on evolution, genetics, psychology and the human species and the effects in our society today.

www.MindStrength.info

We would be delighted for our reader's feedback on this book: By either posting a review on Amazon.com or Amazon.co.uk or email us at: mervyn@mindstrength.info or visit our website www.mindstrength.info

To book or learn about our:

- Speaking Engagements
- Seminars
- Problem Solving Workshops

Email us at: mervyn@mindstrength.info

Mind Strength International
For a clearer perspective
& a brighter future...

111

15476898R00065

Printed in Poland
by Amazon Fulfillment
Poland Sp. z o.o., Wrocław